THE METHOD OF THEOLOGICAL STUDY

THE METHOD OF THEOLOGICAL STUDY

presented in public lectures at the University of Jena in 1617

by Johann Gerhard,

Doctor of Sacred Theology
and Professor at the University of Jena

with the grace and privilege of the sacred imperial majesty
at the expense of Philipp Fuhrmann

published in Jena by Georg Sengenwald
1654

Translated by Paul A. Rydecki

✦ REPRISTINATION PRESS ✦
MALONE, TEXAS

A translation of *Methodus Studii Theologici, publicis praelectionibus in Academia Jenensi Anno 1617 exposita a Johanne Gerhardo, SS. Theologiae Doctore, & in Academia Jenensi Professore* by Johann Gerhard. Copyright 2017 by Paul A. Rydecki. Published by permission of the translator. No part of this publication may be reproduced, stored in a retrieval system, or transmitted in any form or by any means, electronic, mechanical, photocopying or otherwise without the prior written permission of Repristination Press.

Published in 2017

REPRISTINATION PRESS

716 HCR 3424 E

MALONE, TEXAS 76660

www.repristinationpress.com

ISBN 1-891469-75-4

TABLE OF CONTENTS

6

Preface.

To the magnificent, most noble, most excellent hero, Lord Günther Heinrich Plathner, well-known to Jesus Christ, trusted court counselor, etc., of Lord Wilhelm, Duke of Saxony, Jülich-Cleves-Berg, etc., and also the most worthy advisor of the ecclesiastical proto-synod which is in Vinaria:

In always attending to my lord and father-in-law with filial obedience, I wish you enduring happiness!

"If foreign praises are wont to be received poorly by impartial ears, how difficult it is for the speech of one who discusses himself or the members of his own family to seem not to annoy! For if we envy the honor itself, even more do we envy the forth telling of one's glory."*

This prudent warning was recently impressed on my heart by that brilliant writer whom we know to have been a source of joy to Emperor Trajan. This is why I was immediately afraid that it would be difficult for me to keep my words from annoying, even if I only enumerate historically in this Preface to the *Method of Theological Study*, the painstaking efforts of my blessed father, which I am indeed confident that those who take an interest in Sacred Theology can use with benefit. But love for the public good has cast out this fear, and it has pleased

---

*   Pliny the Younger, Letters, Volume 1, #8.

me finally to gratify the desire of my friends, and indeed, the will of several patrons who have wanted such a syllabus to exist for a long time. I will report briefly, therefore, with which writings my father busied himself in each year of the theological curriculum to promote the course of the students of theology.

That I am promoting such a discourse with you, O magnificent hero, will surely surprise no one who has considered your singular and acknowledged favor with which you pursue our theological studies, and who has learned at the same time that you do not wish to soften these rather serious public affairs with any other charms than by seriously rendering or by benevolently hearing the responses on theological matters, if something has been advanced to the middle by those who have surrendered their life to sacred studies.

Therefore, to the theological candidate my father faithfully commends the need for prayer before all things. He himself excelled in this area, both piously and zealously, surpassing not only those who take an interest in theology, but all Christians everywhere. He demonstrated the right path in that book of *Meditationum Sacrarum* that has been translated into so many languages, to which the *Exercitium Pietatis Quotidianum** can be added. That edition of these little books practically seizes from the rest the prize which the Elzevirii of Amsterdam gave to their own brilliant publications.

To pious prayer is to be joined the cursory reading of the Bible, by which he understands that which is done in Latin,

---

*   Published by Repristination Press in an English translation as *The Daily Exercise of Piety.* (1994). [ed.]

or even in the vernacular. Among the German versions, since he especially commends Blessed Luther's translation, therefore, by command of the most illustrious Duke Ernst, that most religious prince, he himself illustrated this version, in part, with a continuous paraphrase and exposition; in part, he recognized that which was illustrated by other learned men with untiring zeal, of which matter Dr. Glassius is witness in the *Bibliorum Vinariensium sive Ernestinorum praefatione*. He further advises that the more notable passages of Holy Scripture are to be underlined in that cursory reading (*Meth. Theol. stud.* part. 3. c. 3.). He provided a useful service in this matter with a German book entitled *Gülden Kleinod*, in which the more notable passages of Holy Scripture are recognized, being drawn together in an elegant order.

To the cursory reading of the Bible he wishes the more accurate reading of the same to be added, for which study, in addition to the painstaking efforts of other Doctors, his own notes and *Commentaria* can serve: In *Genesin, Deuteronomium, priora epistolae ad Romanos capita*, utramque epistolam ad Timotheum, epistolam ad Ebraeos, utramque epistolam Petri, et Apocalypsin D. Johannis**. All of these are available for sale here in Jena and in Erfurt, except for that one commentary on Deuteronomy which has been completed, but not released. It has not yet been published, but it will be shortly.

---

*   Published by Repristination Press in an English translation as *Annotations on the First Six Chapters of St. Paul's Epistle to the Romans (2014).* [ed.]

**   Published by Repristination Press in an English translation as *Annotations on the Revelation of St. John the Theologian (2016).* [ed.]

The *Harmoniae Evangelicae Continuatio* can also be added to the exegetical writings*, together with the *Historia Passionis et Resurrectionis Christi*.** This whole work was previously contained in four volumes, but it has been newly published in Frankfurt in a larger format, at the expense of the Herteliani.

But he also wants a certain synopsis of the entire heavenly doctrine to be put down in a little book and in the memory right away in the first year of theological study (*Methodi Stud. Theol. l. c. C. 5.*). The *Aphorismi Theologici*, which he published as both Theoretical and Practical (printed at Jena in eight volumes, at Wittenberg in four), can serve in place of this little book.

In the second year of theological study, he proposes that an accurate knowledge of theological topics should be imbibed by the mind, for which his *Disputationes Isagogicae LL. Theolog.* can serve. And they could have served better, if his premature death had not begrudged us the continuation of this work.

He recommends for the third year that disputations be instituted, and especially against the papists. In this matter, he proved his own zeal, both by the disputations by which he attacked the *Dogmata Papalia* and by his *Phosphori Pontificii Refutatione*, and also *Bellarmino Orthodoxias teste*, or thirty disputations in which Bellarmine is shown to have proven the articles of our religion. But this was only a prelude to his lengthy work

---

* This work is being published in an English translation by the Center for the Study of Lutheran Orthodoxy.

** Published in an English translation by Repristination Press as *An Explanation of the History of the Suffering and Death of our Lord Jesus Christ* (1998). [ed.]

entitled *Confessio Catholica*, for sale in four volumes by Enderus Noribergae. The German treatises *De Baptismo et S. Coena*[*] can be added to these, which were printed at Jena in four volumes many years ago.

In the fourth year, he wishes not only for the tasks already mentioned to be continued, but also for the *Controversias* to be studied which have arisen *cum Calvinianis Photinianisque*. He wanted to take up this study by means of the academic disputations, some of which he himself developed, and some of which were written down by others and defended by the president. Two volumes were published concerning these, entitled *Disputationum Academicarum*, published in eight volumes (for which I will see to it that the third part will be added soon, and the whole work will again appear in four volumes), *Collegium Antiwendelianum, Disputationes Elenchticae in Evangelia Dominicalia*, likewise *Aphorismi Theologici in Genesin, Amosum, Johannem.*

But the most important thing to read this year will be *Locorum Theologicorum Tomos novem cum Exegesi*. Zacharias Hertelius, the bookseller from Hamburg and a most excellent man, is already overseeing the publication of this book in larger format in Frankfurt, which has enriched it in no small way. Eventually a posthumous treatise will also be made available entitled *Contra Chiliastarum opiniones*, which has been delayed for certain reasons until now. But since he also wanted the practice of church sermons to be begun in this fourth year of theological study, it will be worth it, in my opinion, to read the *Postillam*

[*]   Published in an English translation by Repristination Press as *A Comprehensive Explanation of Holy Baptism and the Lord's Supper* (1996). [ed.]

*Germanicam**, which appeared in previous years both in four volumes and in loose-leaf format. One will also not be sorry if he reads Homiliarum Academicarum in Evang. Domin. et Fest., which have been published here in three parts, available in four volumes and in eight volumes.

I hope it will aid the preacher greatly to read the five books in German entitled *Scholae Pietatis*****, of which various are available for purchase, with the latest edition in four volumes, printed by Enderus. The careful reader may also add to these the *Postillam Salomonaeam*, which Georgius Sengenwaldius had printed here sometime last year in an elegant typeset.

Finally, to all these homiletical writings the future candidate for ministry will certainly not hesitate to add the *Constitutionem Ecclesiasticam*, which was conscripted by order of the illustrious Prince Johann Casimir, Duke of Jülich-Cleves-Berg, etc., that it might be completed in Heldburg at the expense of the superintendent. The *Conciones Passionales* may also be brought into this year, which were printed here last year, followed also by the *Enchiridion Consolatorium contra tentationes mortis*, printed in Latin and German.

My blessed father urges in the present *Method* that the fifth year of theological study should be devoted to the reading

---

* Volume 1 of the *Postilla* was published by the Center for the Study of Lutheran Orthodoxy in an English translation in 2003. An English translation of Volume 2 of the *Postilla* was published by Repristination Press in 2007.

** The first three volumes of an English translation of the *Schola Pietatis* have been published by Repristination Press. The remaining two volumes are forthcoming.

of Blessed Luther, the Fathers, and the Scholastics. *Patrologia* points out in what century this or that Greek or Latin Father lived, what documents he left behind, which writings are genuine and which are counterfeit. But this work is incomplete, nor was it destined by the author for the winepress. But having been convinced by the pleas of my friends not to delay its publication any longer, I committed it to publication a few months ago.

These are the things with which the author powerfully and painstakingly labored to promote the efforts and the curriculum of the candidate of theology for each year of theological study. I also have no doubt that, with the Lord's blessing, my father's labors have produced abundant fruit in the Lord's vineyard, and so I have chosen not to thwart the desire of the good men who have been asking me to put together a catalogue of his published writings. It will be a tremendous aid to this decision I have made, and I, too, will be greatly confirmed in my attempt to aid the studies of others with my little work, when I learn that you, O most excellent patron, have cast the white stone to my purpose.

You have publicly testified, O magnificent hero, that you not only hold dear the writings of my father, but that you have also esteemed them for many years now. Therefore, I hope it will not seem burdensome for you to see an index of those works in this brief listing.

I think it is hardly necessary to point out at length the aim of this little book of his, even as I do not think it necessary to express the reason why I have decided in this place to offer you, O magnificent hero, the small little present of this book as a gift. It was customary among the Romans that, on the kalends of January, the dependents of a patron would send gifts. Although this custom has been repealed by law in the *Ecclesiastical Constitutions* due to the use and abuse of the pagans, who also indulged in such things during the kalends of January, serious men justly think it should be retained.

You, O magnificent hero, became the patron of my studies ten years ago by the supreme Judge of things, but most recently you have also become my father-in-law. You have always shown me the affection of my father, and you show it still now. I will hardly avoid the blemish of an ungrateful man if I do not publicly confess that you recently bound me to yourself with the greatest possible benefits. And though to repay them is beyond my powers, yet I am surely bound to confess that I cherish you as a patron, and that I rightfully report the large amount of help I have received from you in my studies. Hardly two years ago I returned from Belgium and from the Gallic lands and greeted the house of my father after nearly six years of voluntary exile, and behold! You immediately, together with others noble and magnificent leaders of the most illustrious halls of Saxony, thought to have regard for my studies, such as they were. As a result, when those foster-fathers of this university looked with a gracious spirit on my small status and my studies, a public professorship was assigned to me, and at the same time I was granted a place among so many brilliant men, with whom our Salana abounds. But how great that benefit truly is, only he can rightly judge who has learned that sweet and honest sentence: It is surely more gratifying to be made equal to the good than to be increased in dignity.

But this is not the place to commemorate your concern and that of the rest of the patrons and public servants; that is, to commemorate the illustrious benefits that have been furnished to my theological studies. The running field would have to be much larger, if I were to recount all such things. Wherefore, O magnificent hero, my lord patron and most venerable father-in-law, I leave you to the most weighty business of your public service, but first I cast my cheerful vote that the Most High God and Ruler of the Republic of the Church would most mercifully deign to provide us with the jewel of safety for a long time to come.

At Jena, by the paternal muse, on the kalends of January, in the year of salvation 1654.

With filial honor and obedience to your most excellent magnificence.

Johann Ernst Gerhard, Doctor and Public Professor.

The Method of Theological Study

Introduction.

It is not our intention in this preface to describe to many people the dignity and utility of theological study, but to prescribe to those who want to consecrate themselves for this study a method of performing and accomplishing it. Speaking concisely and by way of outline, the study of theology is *the remedy for our innate ignorance in spiritual matters and for the inherent disorder in our emotions; the stronghold for the cultivation of holiness and piety; the means for listening to God daily in the Word and for speaking to God daily in prayer; and, finally, a sort of prelude to that most holy and blessed society which we await in heaven.* Its dignity is to be measured from God; its utility from piety; its necessity from our salvation. We do not wish to detract in the least from the honor that is due the remaining disciplines, which are not only useful, but necessary for the success and good order of human life. Nevertheless, we can hardly fail to assert that theology far surpasses all the other [disciplines].

(1) *In certainty of first principles*, since the only proper beginning of theology is the Word of God. Nothing in heaven and earth is firmer than this. Indeed, the Word of God is firmer than heaven and earth (Luke 21:33). The starting points of the other disciplines are λόγος καὶ πεῖρα, the light of na-

ture and experience, which are not only inferior to the light of Scripture and grace in degree, but also in certainty.

(2) *In nobility of object.* Theology deals with the highest mysteries of faith, which lie beyond all the capabilities of human reason. It teaches the doctrine of the essence and will of God, in the salutary knowledge of whom consists eternal life (John 17:3). It sets forth man as an object insofar as he is to be saved. But the other disciplines deal with those things which the keenness of the human mind can grasp, such as matters of politics, physics, etc. They teach the doctrines that are useful and necessary for traversing the course of this life peacefully, honestly, and comfortably. They set forth man as an object insofar as he is considered in civil society in this life.

(3) *In dignity of purpose.* Theology immediately lays out for itself as its task the salvation of the soul, to which end it directs all its axioms and precepts. The other disciplines have set forth as their goals the honor of life and morals in civil conduct, the health of the human body, or other ends that are far inferior to salvation. Lyranus begins his commentary on the Bible with the saying of Gregory (*homil. 35. in Evang.*), "When compared with eternal life, temporal life should be called death rather than life." And from this he concludes that the books written by philosophers, filled with knowledge only for naturally attaining a goal in this temporal life, if compared to the books of Scripture, which is ordered toward the goal of eternal life, should really be called "books of death rather than life."

(4) *From its power to judge the others.* All other disciplines are subordinate to theology, for it judges each one of them while submitting to the judgment of none, nor does it permit the judgment concerning its own principles to be drawn from

those of the other disciplines. The scholastics say: "Theology, as the chief discipline, governs all others and, as the discipline that is already fit for use, uses all others in its own service." Thus theology prevents the Platonic communion, or the license to use artificial tricks, from being approved in political doctrine. Let the same judgment hold true concerning the other human disciplines. Gerson expresses this beautifully (lib. 1. *de consol. Theol.* prosa 1.): "As grace surpasses nature, as a mistress surpasses her servant and a teacher her student, as eternity surpasses time and understanding surpasses reason, as that which is visible surpasses the invisible, so theology surpasses philosophy. It does not reject it, but instead brings it into its service." Likewise, in libr. 3. Prosa 4.: "The theology of Christians decides if the philosophers' doctrines are true, if they are right, if they are salutary, using them according to its own rules and rendering them Catholic. If they are too dark, it illumines them; if they are mixed with harmful errors, it separates the precious from the worthless, retaining this, eliminating that." So then, the principles of theology are altogether primary and supreme and are in no way subordinate to the principles of the other disciplines, while the principles of the other sciences are only primary in their own realm and are subordinate to the principle of theology.

Furthermore, as we are about to teach the method of theology, we do not understand here with this name the archetypal theology in God*; nor the ectypal theology** in Christ the Man, in angels, in the blessed of the other life, which they call the theology of vision; nor do we understand the natural theology of this life; but we are discussing what is referred to

---

* That is, the Triune God's infinite knowledge of Himself. (Editor)

** That is, knowlege of God revealed in His divine Word. (Editor)

as the theology of revelation, which arises from the light of grace in the revealed Word. Nor are we using this term specifically and strictly for the doctrine of the divine nature of Christ, but we are taking it in a general way for the whole system of Christian doctrine. Nor do we understand with this name the kind of knowledge of the Christian faith and religion that is common to all the faithful, but the more accurate and perfect knowledge of the divine mysteries, such as one can have in this life, by which he who is instructed is able to judge theological controversies, affirm the orthodoxy of the heavenly verity, and powerfully convince his adversaries (Titus 1:9). Nor are we dealing here with that extraordinary way of learning theology by which the Prophets and Apostles gained the knowledge of the divine mysteries through the immediate enlightenment and extraordinary divine inspiration of the Holy Spirit, without any human tools or labors. We are dealing, instead, with the ordinary and mediate manner of learning theology which is acquired through the diligent reading of Holy Scripture, pious meditation, attentively listening to one's teachers, and serious prayer, for which a knowledge of the languages in which the Old and New Testaments were written serves as a tool, and a knowledge of the disciplines of the philosophers serves as an aid, as well as other things which will be enumerated below. No one could deny that such a study of theology is very broad and very wide, and thus a certain order is necessary in learning such an abundance of subjects and writings. As in all the other disciplines, so, too, in this most divine science such an order is of the utmost importance. For just as those who have a certain and accurate knowledge of roads and of the potential shortcuts in the roads arrive at their destination more quickly than those who lack the knowledge of the road and wander about through forests, woodlands, and inhospitable habitats of wild beasts, through mountains, through seas, and through rugged places, so those who proceed methodically and treat all things at the proper time arrive at their predetermined goal in the study of theology much more happily and easily than those who are occupied in this important work without any regard for a rational order and without diligently studying the ancient and more recent writings. That golden saying of Seneca applies here, if not elsewhere: "You must linger with certain wise men, if you wish to move something that adheres stubbornly. He who is everywhere is nowhere. He who lives everywhere lives nowhere." We shall prescribe, therefore, a certain order for advancing in theological study. We shall set definite boundaries within which the studies of those who learn ought to be confined at each time. We shall name certain writers whom they should adopt for themselves as tour guides for that particular year of their studies, so that, with the aid of divine grace, they may reach a laudable end. There will be three main parts of this treatise. The first will explain the general requirements which should not only be brought to the beginning of theological study, but should also be observed throughout the course of it and on a continual basis. The second will expound the preliminary teaching prescribed for theological study. The third will set in order the course of study itself and will recall all the things that are required of the candidates for the five-year course in the statutes of the Theological Faculty.

22

PART ONE.

THE GENERAL REQUIREMENTS OF THEOLOGICAL STUDY.

Blessed Luther (*in praefation. tom. 1. oper. Germ. Jen. ex Ps. 119.*) puts together three requirements of theological study, namely: "Prayer, meditation, and temptation. You should know that Holy Scripture is the kind of book that makes foolish the wisdom of all other books, and so you must thoroughly despair of the keenness of your own ability in acquiring the wisdom of this book and, on bended knee, in true humility, pray earnestly to God that through and on account of His beloved Son He would give you the Holy Spirit that He may illumine and direct you and supply the sound understanding of Scripture. Then you should meditate, that is, ponder the Holy Scripture with utmost zeal and meditate on it inwardly in your heart, not for a moment entertaining that perverse notion that it were enough to read it once, twice, or three times. Then comes temptation, which is like a Lydian stone, for it teaches not only to know, but also to feel and to experience the certainty, truth, gentleness, efficacy, and consolation of the Word, etc." To these three subjects Luther eruditely recalls the things which the royal musician broadly treats in all of Psalm 119 concerning the study of the divine law. (Luther discusses reading and meditation and how important it is in *tom. 5. Jen.*

f. 125. in enarr. Ps. 117 & tom. 8, f. 43., etc.) But since meditation pertains to the third part, and since temptation consists
in the entire praxis about which a warning will be issued in the
coronis at the end of this treatise, something must be said here
about the first aid to theological study, namely, *prayer.* To this,
for the sake of greater clarity and fuller explanation, we will
add two other requirements which should be commended to
the sincere, pious, and divinely instructed theologian as highly
necessary—no less than prayer itself. We say, therefore, not
only at the beginning, but also throughout the entire course
of theological study, that there are three things required of everyone:

1. *The duty of right intention.*
2. *The genuine zeal for piety.*
3. *The task of devout prayer.*

CHAPTER 1.

THE DUTY OF RIGHT INTENTION.

With the phrase 'right intention' we mean here that whoever applies his mind to theological study should have as his goal neither honors, nor riches, nor idle leisure, nor any fleeting, earthly benefits, but only the glory of God alone, the edification of the Church, [and] the salvation of himself and of his neighbor. And he should seek the glory of God with all his heart and with all his soul. In Matthew 6:22, Christ says: "The eye is the lamp of the body. If therefore your eye is simple, your whole body will be full of light. But if your eye is bad, your whole body will be dark." Commenting on these words, Augustine writes (lib. 4. *contra Julianum* cap. 3.):"Recognize this eye as the intention with which each one does what he does, and through this, learn that he who does not do good works with the intention of faith, that is, the faith that works through love—it is as if the whole body which corresponds to those works, as members, is darkness, that is, full of the blackness of sins." Gregory agrees with this (*lib. 28. moralium cap. 13.*): "What is meant by 'eye,' if not the intention of the heart that precedes its work? Before it exercises itself in action, it already contemplates that which it desires. And what is designated as 'the body,' but each and every action that follows its intention as its eye that sees. Whenever it something is done from a perverse intention, even if it is thought to glimmer before men, it is obscured in the examination of internal Judge, etc. In all our works, then, our intention must be weighed with vigilant care, so that, in what it does, it longs for nothing temporal, but fixes itself wholly on the solid foundation of eternity." Therefore, this right intention which issues forth through effective love from true faith in Christ and has as its singular purpose the glory of God alone and the salvation of the neighbor, is required in all our works, but especially in the choice of, and continuation in, theological study. (1) So that all the labors that we undertake therein may be works that are favorable to God and an act of worship that pleases Him. "If right intention is lacking, they can no longer be considered good works," says Augustine (*lib. de opr. Monach.* cap. 26). (2) Whoever seeks, in the study of theology, the honors of the world, transitory riches, the favors of rulers, meager human glory, etc., is easily diverted from a mental state of tranquility and is rendered too casual in the course of his studies and vocation if troubles occur, if he is overwhelmed by the world's hatred, if he is slashed by harsh words, if he is pressed with anxiety over his property. (3) Those whose minds are set ablaze with the firebrands of ambition, greed, envy, etc., disturb the Church with their unnecessary arguments so that they may work for their own honor. They bend doctrine as they please—or to please their rulers—in order to gain wealth for themselves or to quietly enjoy the wealth they have accumulated. Against such men, the Apostle pronounces a grave sentence in Galatians 1:10: "If I were still pleasing men," that is, if I were eager to please them, "I would not be a servant of Christ." (4) Without this right intention, the remaining requirements for theological study cannot be fulfilled; namely, a genuine zeal for piety, serious prayers, and meditation that is pious and favorable to God.

Chapter 2.

The Genuine Zeal for Piety.

Although a zeal for piety is certainly required of all Christians, it is required above all and in a special way of those who have dedicated themselves to theology. And whether they aspire to the ecclesiastical ministry or already function within it, there must flourish in them an integrity of life, moral honesty, and a serious and genuine piety. (1) "The fear of the Lord is the beginning of wisdom," says the royal musician (Psa. 111:9), which his son, the wise King Solomon, repeats in Proverbs 1:7 and 9:10. Therefore, where there is no true fear of God, which is the foundation of genuine piety, there can be no true and heavenly wisdom. (2) James 3:15 distinguishes between *spiritual and carnal* wisdom. He calls spiritual wisdom that which "comes down from above" and describes it as "pure, peaceable, gentle, compliant, full of mercy and good fruits, without partiality and without hypocrisy." He calls carnal wisdom that which is "earthly, natural, and demonic." Therefore, where these fruits and the properties attributed to heavenly wisdom do not appear, heavenly wisdom itself cannot exist. (3) "Into the malevolent soul wisdom will not enter, nor will it dwell in the body that is subject to sin," says the author of the book of Wisdom, chapter 1, verse 4. Therefore, where dominion is granted to sin, there one hopes in vain for the acquisition of heavenly wisdom. (4) The Holy Spirit is that true and internal Teacher who "leads into all truth"(John 16:13, 1 John 2:27). "He who teaches within has His throne in heaven." But He does not dwell in the heart that is subject to sin. (5) He who walks in the darkness of sin and loves the same cannot aspire to the light of spiritual knowledge, wherefore the Apostle pronounces the grave sentence in 2 Cor. 4:4, that the god of this age "blinds the minds of unbelievers," namely, of those who love the darkness of sin, "lest the illumination of the Gospel of the glory of Christ shine on them." (6) True theology consists in *emotion*[*] rather than in *bare knowledge*. *Scal. ex. 148. sect. 4* affirms that "we are more similar to God Most High in kindness than in wisdom." "They profess to know God, but they deny Him with their deeds," says the Apostle concerning the pseudo-theologians and false Christians in Titus 1:16, from which one must clearly conclude that the true and salutary knowledge of God consists not only in words, but in deeds, not only in the confession of the mouth, but also in the emotions of the heart and in the execution of the work. (7) "Awake, you who sleep, rise from the dead and Christ will give you light," says the Apostle in Ephesians 5:14. Therefore, there can be no true and salutary illumination in those who, oppressed by lethargy of soul, delight in the dead works of sin. (8) "The world cannot accept the Spirit of truth" (John 14:17). Indeed, "everything that is in the world is the lust of the flesh, the lust of the eyes, and the pride of life" (1 John 2:16). Therefore, where one still indulges in such things, there the Spirit of truth cannot be. Moses could not approach God until he first took off his sandals (Exodus 3:5). The people of Israel were not allowed to hear the Law until after their purification and preparation (Exodus 19:10). So, let the student of theology take off the garments of the Old

---

[*]   *in affectu*

Adam. (9) True faith is "efficacious through love" (Gal. 5:6). It "overcomes the world" (1 John 5:4). It "purifies hearts" (Acts 15:9). It makes us "one spirit with God" (1 Cor. 6:17), "a new creation in Christ" (2 Cor. 5:17). It causes Christ to dwell in our hearts (Eph. 3:17). Therefore, where there is no love, nor victory over the world, nor purity of heart, nor inner renewal and union with Christ, there also true faith cannot abide. Nevertheless, we must caution that all these things are to be understood with the added distinction between knowledge *of the letter and of the Spirit*, between faith as it is considered *as a matter of knowledge and as a matter of trust*, between *historical and saving* faith, between sins *of weakness and sins that dominate*, etc. (10) Finally, the apostolic admonitions concerning zeal for piety must be applied to the ministers of the Church. Paul writes in 1 Tim. 1:18, "I commit this charge to you, O Timothy, according to the prophecies previously made about you, that by them you may wage the good warfare," v. 19, "holding onto faith and a good conscience." 1 Tim. 3:2: "A bishop must be irreproachable, sober, wise, etc." 1 Tim. 4:7: "Exercise yourself in piety." 1 Tim. 4:12: "Be an example to the believers in word, in behavior, in love, in spirit, in faith, in chastity." 2 Tim. 2:22: "Flee the desires of youth, and pursue righteousness, faith, love, and peace." Titus 1:7: "A bishop must be blameless, as a steward of God." 1 Peter 5:3: "Let them be examples for the flock, etc." Gregory expands on this (lib. 3. *pastoralis curae* cap. 6.): "It is necessary that, if any admonish with the word of holy preaching, they be diligent in zeal for doing good, lest they incite others with their voice to act shamefully by the example of their work. First let them examine themselves through excellent deeds, and then let them render others ready to live well. First let them beat themselves with the wings of reflection. If there is anything in them that is useless, let them reveal it by diligent investigation and correct it with careful attention. Only then let them set in order the lives of others with their speech. First let them take care to punish their own sins with weeping. Then let them denounce those things that should be punished in others. And before they sound the words of exhortation, let them first proclaim everything that they will say with their own works." This means that weight is added to the words of the teachers if those who hear see them confirming by their example the things which they prescribe with their words. Augustine (lib. 4 *de doctr. Christ.* cap. 27.): "In order to be heard with obedience, the life of a teacher has greater weight than any amount of grandeur in his delivery." "Either teach with your character, or not at all. Do not attract people with your words while driving them away with your deeds. Excel in deeds, as you should, and there will be less of a need for speech. A painter teaches better with clearly defined images," as John Damascene says, quoting Gregory Nazianzus (orat. 3. *de Imagine* p. 805). On the other hand, if a person teaches soundly but lives shamefully, then what he offers with one hand he snatches away with the other. What he builds up with one hand he destroys with the other. What he raises up with one hand, he tears down again with the other.

CHAPTER 3.

THE DAILY TASK OF DEVOUT PRAYER.

What we have said about zeal for piety, namely, that it certainly is required of all Christians, but above all and in a special way of theologians, we wish to repeat with regard to the daily exercise of serious and devout prayer. We demonstrate the need for serious prayers in the study of theology with the following foundational principles:

(1) After the Fall, we are all devoid of the image of God, that is, of the light of divine knowledge in the mind and of the conformity with the divine Law in the will, wherefore we are all said to be "darkness" (Eph. 5:8; John 1:5; Acts 26:18); "we have an intellect obscured by darkness" (Eph. 4:18). A heavenly irradiation and illumination is therefore required, which is not obtained except through prayer.

(2) The Scriptures are not understood in a salutary way except through the Holy Spirit, by whose impulse and inspiration they were written. "Flesh and blood do not reveal to us the salvific knowledge of Christ, but the heavenly Father" (Mat. 16:17). "Carnal man does not perceive the things that are of the Spirit of God, for they are foolishness to him and he cannot understand them" (1 Cor. 2:14). "No prophecy of the Scripture is of private interpretation, for prophecy never came

about by human will, but holy men of God spoke, inspired by the Holy Spirit" (2 Pet. 1:20–21). Note here the etiology, that the Scriptures are neither understood nor explained by the human spirit, because they were not written by human will, but by the Holy Spirit. After discussing the prophetic books, Justin submits (*in Dialog. cum Tryph.* p. 173.): "For the Scriptures are not clearly perceived and understood by any, unless God and His Christ grant understanding." Theoph. (*in cap. 10. Joh.*) writes that the Holy Spirit is most likely to be understood as the "Doorkeeper, because the Scriptures which show us the Christ are understood and opened by the Holy Spirit." Damascene (*homil. on the holy Sabbath*, not far from the beginning, p. 184) commands his hearers to pray that they be given "the divine enlightenment of the all-Holy Spirit, apart from whom the wise are made foolish and with whom the unlearned are made far wiser than the wise." Luther says (*de serv. arbitr. tom. 3. Jen.* p. 167): "To be sure, without the Holy Spirit's light, not a single *iota* in the Scriptures is perceived clearly." No one sees the sun without the light of the sun. So no one knows God without God. But the enlightenment of the Holy Spirit is to be obtained through prayer. "The Father will give the Holy Spirit to those who ask" (Luke 11:13). "If anyone lacks wisdom, let him ask of God, who gives abundantly to all and does not reproach, and it will be given to him" (James 1:5).

(3) Through prayers that proceed from faith, that spiritual enlightenment of the mind that is so necessary for understanding the Scripture is not only preserved, but increased. The Spirit of wisdom and understanding departs from those who neglect to pray, wherefore they slip back into their former darkness.

(4) For the salutary understanding and explanation of the Scripture, it is required that we "take captive every thought

and make it obedient to Christ" (2 Cor. 10:5). Here he has fallen down, lest we should impose the thoughts of our reason onto the Scripture and the light of grace, which can only be guarded through prayer. Through prayer, the inner man grows, whose increase means the decrease of the outer man.

(5) Without serious prayer, every work that is undertaken in theological study is not only in vain, but also destructive. For how many have stepped forth, in our memory and in that of the Fathers, who have drawn—or have wanted to appear to have drawn—their poisonous dogmas from the wholesome and beautiful flowers of the Scripture, with which they afterwards horribly infected whole provinces, whole kingdoms? What other cause was there of this evil, but that they were devoid of sincere love for God and of serious piety and so did not ask that their studies be divinely ruled? But, having trusted merely in human wisdom and eloquence, they ruined themselves and others. Any theologian who does not arm himself with prayer against the devil becomes the devil's own instrument of deception and seduction.

(6) "Blessed is he who turns the Scriptures into deeds," say the ancients. "If you know these things," says Christ to the disciples whom he was shaping in zeal for the heavenly doctrine, "blessed are you if you do them" (John 13:17). Where there is a greater gift of knowledge, there transgression is exposed to greater guilt. Knowledge of the divine will damns itself all the more unless the execution of the work is added. The Rabbis say: "Be wise in deeds, not words. For the wisdom that is in deeds will profit you in the future age, but that which is in words only remains here." Now, the Scriptures cannot be turned into deeds except by the Holy Spirit's divine grace and efficacy, which cannot exist in us without prayer. The streams

of divine grace do not descend upon us except through the channels of faithful prayer. Luther says, "He who prays diligently has completed half of his studies."

(7) This is why the holy men of God have sought from God the true understanding of Scripture with such serious and ardent prayers. David, the royal Prophet, continually pondered the book of the divine law and "meditated on it day and night" (Psalm 1:2). Nonetheless, he asks repeatedly in Psalm 119 for divine illumination, and with the most emphatic words. Verse 10: "Lord, I have sought You with my whole heart. Do not permit me to stray from Your commandments." Verse 12: "Teach me Your statutes." Verse 18: "Open my eyes and I will consider the wondrous things of Your law." Verse 19: "I am a pilgrim on the earth. Do not hide from me Your commandments." Verse 27: "Instruct me in the way of Your precepts, and I shall train in all Your wondrous works." Verse 33: "Teach me, O Lord, the way of Your precepts, and I will observe it unto the end." Verse 34: "Give me understanding and I shall search Your law and guard it in my heart." Verse 66: "Teach me good understanding and knowledge, for I trust in Your commandments. Verse 73: "Give me understanding, that I may learn Your commandments." Verse 125: "I am Your servant; give me understanding, that I may know Your testimonies." Verse 130: "The declaration of Your words enlightens and gives understanding to the simple." Verse 135: "Shine Your face upon Your servant and teach me Your statutes." Verse 169: "Let my cry come before You, O Lord. According to Your word, give me understanding." Wisdom 9:10: "Send Your wisdom, O Jehovah, from Your holy heaven, from the throne of Your greatness, that it may be with me and work with me, that I may know what is acceptable to You." In Matthew 13:36, the disciples approach Christ and ask

Him for the interpretation of His words, saying: "Explain the parable to us." In Revelation 5:9, the twenty-four elders, representing the state of the Church Triumphant and Militant, sing a new song, saying to the Lamb: "Worthy are You to receive the book and to open its seals, etc." Origen interprets this (*Homil. 17. in Exodum*) to mean that we are to ask God to open the sealed book, that is, the mysteries of His word, through Christ and for His sake, who already long ago "opened His disciples' mind that they might understand the Scriptures" (Luke 24:45). To this pertain the forms of prayer that occur in the ecclesiastical writings, some of which we will refer to here.

Hilary prays in this way (toward the end of *lib. 1. de Trinit.* p. 12.): "I know, O Father, Almighty God, that I owe You, as the chief duty of my life, the praise of my every word and sense. For the use of this gift of speech, which You have granted me, can bring no greater reward than that it may serve You by proclaiming You—You and what You are, Father of God the Only-begotten—and revealing You either to the world that does not know You or to the heretic who denies You. And yet, this is only the expression of my own will. I must also pray for the gift of Your help and mercy, that with the breath of Your Spirit You would fill the sails of our faith and confession which are spread wide to You, and that You would propel us on the course of the preaching that has begun. For the Author of that faithful promise to us is not unfaithful when He says, 'Ask, and it shall be given to you; seek and you will find; knock and it will be opened to you.' We poor men will ask for those things which we need, and we will employ steadfast zeal in searching the words of Your Prophets and Apostles, and we will knock on all the doors of locked understanding. But it is Yours to bestow that which we ask and to provide that which we seek and to open when we knock. For we are dull with the lazy numbness of our nature, and we are confined by the feebleness of our natural state to understanding Your affairs within the necessity of ignorance. But the study of Your doctrine prepares us for the understanding of divine knowledge, and the obedience of faith carries us beyond natural thought. We therefore look to You to arouse the beginnings of this fearful undertaking and to confirm them with growing success, and that we may grasp the words of the Spirit, either of the prophetic or the apostolic band, in no other sense but that in which they themselves spoke, and follow the properties of their words with the same meanings, etc. Grant us, therefore, the meaning of the words, the light of understanding, a regard for the sayings and a true faith, and grant also that, as we believe, we may also speak."

Ephrem the Syrian uses this form of prayer (*apud Maximum Scriptorem Graecum*): "O Lord Jesus Christ, open the ears and the eyes of my heart that I may hear and understand Your words and do Your will. I am a stranger on the earth. Do not hide Your commandments from me. Open my eyes and I will contemplate the wonders of Your Law."

Nazianzus: "Supply grace, O Christ, to my labors."

The prayer of Augustine which he used to say after every treatise: "Having turned to the Lord God, the Almighty Father, with a pure heart, let us give Him true and highest thanks, as we are able in our humble state, asking Him with our whole spirit for His singular clemency, that He would deign to hear our prayers in His good-pleasure, that He would also drive the enemy away from our thoughts and actions by His power, multiply faith unto us, govern our mind, grant us spiritual thoughts and guide us to His blessedness, through Jesus Christ, His Son, our Lord, who lives and reigns with Him in the unity of the Holy Spirit, God for all the ages of ages. Amen."

This is another prayer of Augustine (lib. 11. *Confess.* cap. 2.): "O Lord my God, be attentive to my prayer, and let Your mercy hear my desire, for it burns not for me alone, but wants to be profitable to brotherly love. And You see in my heart that it is so, that I would sacrifice to You the service of my mind and tongue. Give that which I offer You. For I am poor and lowly. You are rich toward all who call upon You, who, free from care, bear the care of us all. Circumcise my lips, within and without, from all temerity and from every lie. Let Your Scriptures be my pure delights, that I may neither be mistaken in them nor deceive from them. O Lord, attend to my cry and have mercy on me, O Lord my God, Light of the blind and Strength of the weak, and also Light of the seeing and Strength of the strong, attend to my soul and hear me crying from the depths. For if Your ears are not also present in the depths, where shall we go, where shall we cry? Yours is the day and Yours is the night. At Your command, the moments flee. Grant space therefrom for our meditations on the hidden things of Your Law, nor close it toward those who knock. For You also did not wish for the dark secrets of so many pages to be written in vain, nor are those forests devoid of their deer that retire into them and refresh and walk and feed, lie down and ruminate. O Lord, perfect me and reveal them to me. Behold, Your voice is my joy, Your voice surpasses an abundance of pleasures. Give that which I love, for I do love, and this You have given. Do not forsake Your gifts, and do not spurn Your thirsty grass. Let me confess to You whatever I find in Your books and hear the voice of praise and drink You in and consider the wonders of Your Law from the very beginning, when You made heaven and earth, until Your eternal reign of Your holy city. O Lord, have mercy on me and hear my desire, for I esteem that which is not of the earth, not of gold and silver or of precious stones, not of fancy clothes, or of honors and powers, or of carnal pleasures, or of the needs of the body and of our pilgrimage through this life, all of which are added to us who seek Your kingdom and Your righteousness. See, O Lord my God, where my desire comes from. The unrighteous have told me of delights, but not such as Your Law, O Lord. Behold, where does my desire come from? See, Father! Look and see and approve and may it be pleasing in the sight of Your mercy that I may find grace in Your presence, that the inward parts of Your words may be opened to me as I knock. I beseech through our Lord Jesus Christ, Your Son, the Man of Your right hand, the Son of Man, whom You established for Yourself as Your Mediator and ours, through whom You sought us who were not seeking You, and yet You sought us that we might seek You; Your Word, by which You made all things, including me; Your only Word by which You called into adoption the people of believers, including me; through Him I beseech You, who sits at Your right hand and entreats You on our behalf, in whom are hidden all the treasures of wisdom and knowledge. These I seek in Your books."

Fulgentius (lib. 1. *de praedestinatione ad Monimum*, right at the beginning of pag. 7) piously writes in this way: "This I do not cease to ask of our true Lord and Master Jesus Christ, that, either through the words of the Scriptures, or through the speech of my brothers and fellow disciples, or even through the inner and more delightful teaching of His inspiration (where, without the sound of words and without letters, the truth speaks the more sweetly and secretly), He might deign to teach me those things which I so propose, so assert, that in my propositions and assertions I may ever hold fast to the truth (which neither deceives nor is deceived), ever be found obedient and consenting. For, that I may be able to obey and consent to the truth, the Truth itself illuminates, the Truth itself gives aid, the Truth itself confirms. I ask of this Truth that I may be taught many things which I do not know, from which I have received a few things which I know. I ask this Truth, with mercy going before and after, to teach me the things I do not know but that are beneficial to know. In these which I know to be true, may He guard me. In the things in which I, as a man, am deceived, let Him correct me. In the true things in which I falter, may He confirm me. And from false and harmful things, may He rescue me, that in all my thoughts and words, which He wholesomely gives, He may find and cause to proceed from my mouth those things which are chiefly favorable before Him and which thus become acceptable to all the faithful."

Here is a prayer of Thomas Aquinas: "O ineffable Creator, my Lord and my God, who are said to be the true Fountain of light and wisdom and the preeminent beginning, deign to pour out the radiance of Your brightness upon the darkness of my understanding, removing from me the twofold darkness— the sin and ignorance in which I was born. You who create the eloquent tongues of babes, instruct my tongue, and pour out upon my lips the grace of Your benediction. Give me the acuity to understand, the ability to retain, the subtlety to interpret, the facility to teach and the abundant grace to speak. Direct my coming in and perfect my going out, through Christ our Lord."

Our Luther (Tom. 1. *Epistol. ad Spalatinum*) offers this form of prayer, brief but pious: "O Lord God, if it should please

You to accomplish something through me, for Your glory, not mine, nor for the glory of any man, mercifully grant me a true understanding of Your words." And he prescribes this form of prayer to the students of theology in a prayer for the priestly life: "O Lord, give me to understand these things rightly, and more, to do them. Behold, O Most Excellent Lord Jesus, if this study is not for Your glory, do not cause me to understand even a syllable. But give me as much as You see fit for Your glory, etc." Many forms of prayer like these can be collected by those who are zealous for piety and can be incorporated here. But such prayers should normally be used by them at the ordinary hour of prayer, both at Matins and at Vespers, and certainly the beginning of any labor should be commended to God by serious prayer.

Part Two.

The Preliminary Teaching Prescribed for the Study of Theology.

J ust as the temple in Jerusalem was constructed in such a way that, in the first place, there was an *outer vestibule* or *court of the Gentiles*; in the second place, a *court of the Jews, a great court, an earthly sanctuary* also called the *portico of Solomon;* and finally in the third place, *a holy place or sanctuary, a court of the priests, also called the inner court,* which contained the *Holy of Holies* in the inmost room, into which the High Priest alone would enter once a year, where no one could enter except through the court of the Gentiles and the earthly sanctuary; so, too, no one can enter into the innermost shrines and chambers of learning theology in the ordinary way, but only through a certain vestibule, namely, through the studies of languages and the liberal arts. And just as in the great court or the second part of the temple there was placed a *bronze sea* called a brim, supported by twelve oxen, and likewise a *bronze bowl,* a vessel filled with a large capacity of water (1 Kings 7:23, 2 Chr. 4:2) in which the priests would wash their hands and feet when they were about to enter the sanctuary, so, too, it is not fitting for future theologians to invade the sanctuary of the Lord with dirty hands and feet, but with the studies of the languages and the arts, like first washing away an innate stain at the fountain of Helicon. The people of Jerusalem, who lived in the kingdom's capital, the seat of the priesthood and the public University of the whole world, in addition to the temple of divine revelation and the office of worship, had several *schools* (the Rabbis count 431) in which divine and human wisdom was passed on, as can be gathered from Acts 6:9. Melanchthon compares the studies of languages and the arts to the *baskets* in which the pieces of bread were ordered to be collected and stored (Mat. 14:20), since they are the tools by which the heavenly doctrine can be properly passed on, propagated to posterity, and defended against adversaries. The history of the Church is a witness to the fact that the contempt for languages and liberal studies brought along with it the corruption of doctrine under the papacy. It was for this reason that, at the very beginning of God's wondrous work of Reformation, it was decided that the studies of languages and the arts would begin to flourish again in our Germany.

SECTION 1: THE KNOWLEDGE OF LANGUAGES.

We are told in Genesis 11 that all the earth was once "of one lip and speech," that is, of *one* language, but that a confusion of languages arise from the arrogance of the architects of the Tower of Babel, which God, in His righteous judgment, decided to punish with this confusion. (Philastrius [*de haeres.* cap. 106.] errs greatly when he contends that there were many languages from the very beginning, and he says it is heretical if anyone should say that there was only one language before the Tower of Babel was built.) It can be confirmed with many arguments that the primeval language common to all men before that confusion of tongues was Hebrew, especially by studying the names of our first parents and of the Patriarchs, of rivers, of peoples and nations, and also by the nomenclature of their animals, of which there are still some traces in other languages. The ancient writer Berosus clearly testifies that the antediluvian earth was called 'Arez,' and fire was called, 'Esch,' which are the very same Hebrew words still in use to this day. Jerome writes (in cap. 3. *Soph.*): "The Hebrew language is earlier and older than the other languages in such a way that it is the mother of all languages. It is intermixed and practically interspersed in all of them, so that there is no tribe, no language so foreign and so far away from the Hebrew usage that it does not retain some maternal, that is, Hebrew, vocables, whether whole or corrupt." And Försterus writes in the preface of his Hebrew lexicon, that "remarkable glory and good fortune belong to the Hebrew language, for it neither begs nor borrows anything from other languages, while the others borrow many words from it." This clearly argues for the primeval antiquity of this language, so that the counsel and judgment of the Egyptian pharaoh Psammetichus is justly ridiculed, who, as Herodotus reports in his second book, wanting to know which language was the most ancient of all, gave two babies to a shepherd to be brought up, giving strict orders that no one was to speak a single word in their hearing, but that they were to be nursed in a certain isolated cottage at the teats of she-goats. But when the time came in which boys otherwise begin to talk, they uttered the word *beccus*, from the sound of the goats, which means 'bread' in the Phrygian tongue. The pharaoh therefore concluded that the Phrygian language is the most ancient and natural to man. (Theodoret (*q. 60. in Gen.*) asserts that the Syriac language was the vernacular for Adam and the other Fathers, and that Hebrew was only used in sacred rites and reserved for books. But he is refuted by Genesis 31:46. Salicaeus, archbishop of Toledo, suggests that Gothic letters were the first of all.) Goropius is also justly ridiculed, who, by certain etymological contortions of the names given to the Patriarchs, wanted to claim the glory of antiquity for the Belgic language, although this glory only fits with the Hebrew tongue. In that confusion of languages at Babel and in the dispersion of the nations, the integrity of the Hebrew language was preserved in the family of Heber, from whom also the Hebrew appellation was undoubtedly derived. (The Hebrew language is called (1) *Judean* [2 Kings 18:28, Isa. 36:11], because it was first used purely by the people of Judea. (2) *Canaanite* [Isa. 19:18], because it was developed and preserved by Abraham the Hebrew, who dwelled among the Canaanites. (3) *The language of holiness or the holy language*, both because in it the mysteries of salvation were handed down to the Patriarchs, and because God Himself used it. (4) *The language of Heber or the Heberian or Hebrew language.* The reason for this has already been explained. (5) In Zep. 3:9 it is called 'a chosen lip,' because the Patriarchs and Prophets used it in their sermons and writings.) Ambrose, on the other hand, thinks that it is called by this name because it is derived from the name of Abraham or *Abrahae*, so that Hebrew or *Ebraeus* is used for *Abraeo*. Others think that it is because the word Hebrew denotes one with is transitory or 'transfluvial,' from the Hebrew word עבר, which means 'he went across.' (Cf. Numbers 24:2.) But Augustine captures the meaning better (lib. 16. *de civit. Dei* cap. 11. in princ.): "Because this language remained in the family of Heber, with the other nations being separated by different languages, it is believed, not without merit, to have been the earlier common language for the human race, and therefore it was called 'Hebrew' thereafter." Eucherius asserts the same thing (lib. 2. *in Gen.* cap. 2.): "At that time, when the division of languages occurred, this language remained solely in the house of Heber, where it had previously been used." Elias Levita testifies that the Hebrew language was also preserved among the people of Israel at the time of the Egyptian slavery and remained the vernacular for them without any change at all until the time of the Babylonian captivity. (He teaches that the Israelites in Egypt retained three things without any change: their family names, their clothing, and their use of the Hebrew language.) And thus God, through Moses and the Prophets, naturally determined to have His words recorded in the Hebrew tongue, because it was the language of the Israelite people, whom He had chosen to be His very own (Deu. 7:6, 14:2, 26:18) and to whom were entrusted those words (Rom. 3:2). It was the familiar and native language which God Himself had used with Adam, the Patriarchs, and

Moses. Therefore, since all the books of the Old Testament were written in Hebrew (except for a few things in Daniel, Ezra, and Jeremiah which were written in Chaldaic), and since this is no longer the vernacular for us as it once was for the Israelites, there is a pressing need for those who desire an accurate knowledge of the prophetic Scripture to learn Hebrew. The Books of the New Testament were written down by the Evangelists and Apostles in Greek, for that language was very common to all the Gentiles at that time, to whom the Apostles were sent out to preach the Gospel. Augustine writes (lib. 8. *de Civ. Dei* cap. 2.): "The Greek language was held to be clearer among the rest of the Gentiles." (Epist. 200.): "This is by far the preeminent language among the Gentiles." (*Cic. pro Archia.*): "Greek literature is read among almost all the Gentiles." Since this language is also not the vernacular among us, it is just as necessary for the future theologian to learn it as it is for him to become well-acquainted with Hebrew. Finally, when the Romans subdued provinces and kingdoms and brought them under Roman rule, they also brought their language into use in those places, and thus many doctors of the Western Church once wrote in Latin, and many authors today have also written their more recent commentaries and books in Latin. Therefore, the theologian cannot fail to know this language, too, especially since it is practically the only language we use in the schools of higher learning for lectures and for disputations.

CHAPTER 1.

THE NECESSITY FOR LEARNING HEBREW.

The absurd constitution of the Tridentine Fathers has already been cast out of the orthodox churches and schools wherein they command (sess. 4. *Conc.*), under the thunderbolt of anathema, that the ancient and conventional Latin edition "be considered authentic in public lectures, disputations, proclamations, and expositions, and that no one should hear it under any pretense or presume to reject it." But it is one thing to mind a prophet, and another to mind a translator, as Jerome, to whom that conventional translation is falsely attributed, correctly writes on the Pentateuch. Therefore, no translation (whichever one it may be), but only the Hebrew text in the Old Testament and the Greek text in the New is the authentic one, nor can anyone refuse to be called back from the little brooks to return to the fountains, that is, from the translations to the original language in which the Prophets and Apostles wrote. (1) Only those languages in the Holy Scriptures are authentic in which the holy men of God wrote the sacred books. But the Prophets in the Old Testament wrote their books in Hebrew and the Apostles in the New Testament wrote their books in Greek. Therefore, the major premise is obviously true, for it certainly cannot be said that what came from the Prophets and Apostles does not precisely agree with the original language.

The translations are like little brooks; the original text is like a fountain. The former are like something that is patterned after a rule or standard, while the latter is like the ruling standard. Judgment should be made about the little brooks on the basis of the fountain; that which is patterned after a rule and standard should obviously be judged by the rule and standard. Here some bring in the passage from Psalm 68:27, "In the congregations, bless the Lord God מִמְּקוֹר," that is, "from the fountains of Israel." Those fountains of Israel are the streams of heavenly doctrine given to the people of Israel in the Hebrew language (Rom. 3:2, Isa. 12:3). (All authentic sacred Scripture is *inspired by God* [2 Tim. 3:16]. The translations are not *inspired by God*. Therefore, they are not authentic. Any monarch wants judgment to be made about the genuine sense of his edicts from the original language of them, not from translations, especially if the translations are corrupt.) (2) The same thing can be confirmed by six hundred sayings of the Fathers. Jerome (*adv. Helvid.* tom. 3.): "It is to be believed that a stream flows much purer from a fountain than from a brook." He says the same thing elsewhere. (*in Epistola ad Suniam et Fretillam*): "Just as in the New Testament we return to the fountain of the Greek word, in which the New Testament was written, so in the Old Testament we return to the Hebrew verity." (*in Epist. ad Vitalem*) "I am accustomed to flee to the Hebrew verity as to a stronghold or to a garrison." (*in epist. ad Lucinium*): "The faith of the old books is to be examined from the Hebrew volumes in such a way that the faith of the new books yearns for the standard of the Greek word." Augustine (lib. 2. *de doctr. Christ.* cap. 11): The men of Latin tongue whom we now receive for instruction need two other languages in order to know the divine Scriptures, namely, Hebrew and Greek, so that they may return to the earlier manuscripts in case the infinite variety of

Latin interpreters causes some doubt." (Libr. 15. *de C. D. c.* 13. circa finem): "When some difference is discovered between two manuscripts and the accounts of the things that have taken place cannot both be true, I have no doubt that the right thing to do is to believe the one that is in the language from which a translation has been made into another language by translators." Hilary on Psalm 118: "We have frequently admonished that a Latin translation is unable to provide a satisfactory understanding." Ambrose (*de incarn. Dom. Sacr.* cap. 8.): "Thus we find in the Greek manuscripts, whose authority is greater." Cassiodus (lib. 1. *Instit.* cap. 15.): "It is fitting that the place from whence the salutary translation has come to us should again be revisited when the proper correction is needed, etc." (3) The more reasonable of our adversaries acknowledge the same thing. For let us overlook the decision of Canon Law (*c. Jejunium* dist. 76.): "We are compelled to return to the Hebrews and seek the truth of the Scripture from the fountain rather than from the brooks," to which the gloss is added, "In doubtful matters, one must return to its origin and believe the Teacher rather than the disciple, etc." * Since this hypothesis stands true and certain, namely, that only the Hebrew text of the Old Testament is authentic and that, in doubtful matters, one can appeal to it over all translations, it is evident how necessary is the study of Hebrew for the future theologian. Nor does that subterfuge have any place here, that there are at hand the most excellent and precise translations of Vatablus, Junius, Tremel-

---

*   Since the saying of Jerome cited a little earlier is alleged by Dist. 9. of the Fathers, see Ludovicus Vives in *comment. lib. 14. de Civ. Dei* cap. 8. lib. 15. ejusd. cap. 11. & 13. Bened. Arias Montanus in *praefat. super opus Biblicum*, Erasmus in *compend. Theologico & praefat. annotat. in N. T.* etc. (Reuchlin, walking in the footsteps of Jerome, says that the Hebrews drink fountains, the Greeks streams, the Latins swamps.)

lius, Santis Pagnini, Münster, Arias Montanus, etc., and Luther's translation is rightly to be preferred to them all. (1) For what will be done if those translations disagree with one another, as often happens? There one must certainly return to the fountains and judge the integrity of the translations from them. (2) If the adversaries reject the authority of those translations, we must necessarily go back to the fountains. (3) No translation can be made so precise that it fully and perfectly expresses the idioms, emphases and emotional forces of the original language. I shall cite a passage from Jamblichus Platonicus concerning this subject: "For names do not entirely preserve the same meaning when translated, but there are certain idioms in each nation which cannot be signified by language to another nation. And, in the next place, even if it were possible to translate them, they no longer preserve the same power when translated. Foreign names, likewise, have much emphasis, much conciseness, and participate of less ambiguity, variety, and richness of vocabulary." If this is true in any other language, it certainly holds true in Hebrew, which takes the prize for vigorous brevity, gravity, and special characteristics. Paulus Fagius (in *praefat. Chald. paraphr.*): "Just as purer water is always drawn from the fountains themselves than from the pools derived from them, so are those things always purer, to some extent, that are drawn from the primary languages themselves in which the oracles of God were passed on to us, as from crystal clear fountains." Although the Evangelists and Apostles of the New Testament wrote in Greek, nevertheless they retain very many Hebrew phrases and idioms which no one could skillfully explain unless he knew Hebrew. (4) It is a miserable thing to look into such a great matter through foreign eyes, especially for him who is appointed to be the eye of others. Indeed, it cannot be done without making many mistakes as one relies on the judgment of others. Therefore, we conclude that the knowledge of Hebrew is necessary for the theologian, that he may be able to approach the Old Testament fountains themselves, investigate the special characteristics and emphases of the words, search for the doctrines that are hidden rather often in a single phrase, explain the text more fully, and refute his adversaries more deliberately. To this pertains the decree of the Council of Vienne convened around the year 1308 under Pope Clement V, that in each of the universities—in Rome, Paris, Oxford, Bologna, and Salamanca—there should be two professors of Hebrew, Arabic and Chaldaic. And the serious exhortation of Dr. Luther (*in comm. Ps. 45. tom. 3. Lat. Jen. f. 462.*): "I have often admonished you to learn Hebrew and not to neglect it so. For even if there were no other use for this language, it ought to be learned as an act of thanksgiving. It shows that a certain part of the religion and worship of God is to teach or to learn this language, which alone is divine, if anything has ever been divine. For in it one hears God speaking; one hears the saints calling upon God and carrying out the greatest deeds, so that the study that is invested into learning this language could rightly be called a sort of Mass or worship of God. Therefore, I earnestly encourage you not to neglect it. For there is a danger, lest God be offended by this ingratitude and deprive us not only of the knowledge of this holy tongue, but also of Greek, Latin, and all of religion. For how easy is it to incite some foreign people so that these languages perish at once? But besides the fact that this study is part of divine worship, it also contains very great utility. For if there are to be any future theologians—as there must be, for we cannot all teach law or medicine—it behooves them to be fortified against the Pope and other loathsome rabble of men who, having uttered a single word of Hebrew, at once imagine themselves to be masters of this holy tongue. And then, if we ourselves have not mastered it, they will mock and ridicule us as a bunch of asses. But if we, too, have been fortified with the knowledge of this language, we will be able to stop their impudent mouths. For thus the devil and his ministers must be resisted. Moreover, I think that we will have enemies of our religion—Spaniards, Frenchman, Italians, and even Turks—among whom a knowledge of Hebrew will certainly be useful, for I know how much it has profited me against my enemies, which is why I would not be without this knowledge—however small it may be—even for infinite sums of gold. And you, too, who will eventually teach the religion, ought to learn this language, if you do not wish to be counted as common cattle and unlearned rabble who teach the Sunday Gospels and the Catechism with the aid of books written in German. But we need some doctrinal leaders. We must have fighters who stand on the battle line against the men of other nations and tongues, men who are teachers, judges, and masters in this language." Thus far Luther.

CHAPTER 2.

THE TOOLS TO BE EMPLOYED IN THE STUDY OF THE HOLY LANGUAGE.

However much it may appear to be foreign to our purpose to discuss the method of learning the holy language, since, as a matter of preliminary teaching, we require that the one to whom we are now prescribing an order for theological study should already know Hebrew, nevertheless it will not be a fruitless or redundant endeavor briefly to discuss here, as an aside, some tools for learning this language.

(1) In the knowledge of this language, one advances further and more swiftly through oral instruction than through the private reading of books.

(2) Among the books of grammar, of which there are many, the books of Mehlfurer, Helvicus, and Buxtorf are seen as preferable to the rest.

(3) Among the Hebrew lexicons, the best are of Pagnini, Förster, Avenarius, and Buxtorf, but the best of the rest is Schindler's *Lexicon Pentaglotton, Hebraicum, Chaldaicum, Syriacum, Talmudico Rabinicum & Arabicum*, printed in Hanover in the year 1612.

(4) With the grammatical lessons and rules should at once be combined the reading of some Biblical writing, espe-

cially from the beginning of the historical writings. Here applies the suggestion that some chapter of grammatical rules should be repeated daily for the student of the holy language, accompanied by the reading of a chapter of the Bible in which the use of those rules is observed.

(5) Of the various editions of the Hebrew Bible, the best one to use is edition of Arias Montanus, which is considered a classic work and is also sold separately. It has the following title: *Biblia Hebraica, eorundem Latina interpretatio Xantis Pagnini Lucensis, recenter Bencd. Ariae Montani et quorundam aliorum studio ad Hebraicam dictionem diligentissime expensa, Antverpiae, Ann. 84.* In that edition, the verses are separated by numbers. The Latin translation of Montanus is written above the Hebrew text. Pagnini's translation and the root words are written in the margin with a little more difficulty, and the Greek New Testament books have been added with a translation at the foot of the page.

(6) There are few root words in the holy language, compared with other languages. (There are about 1,500 root words.) Therefore, as an aid for memory in the course of study, they can comfortably be assigned in alphabetical order; their principal meanings can be attached to them; and they can all be included together on just a few pages, and in this way, they can be reviewed every day.

(7) The general rules concerning the idioms of the holy language should be summarized in simple words and connected phrases. There is great benefit in using these rules in reading and interpreting Scripture.

(8) A more certain and readier knowledge of this language can be attained by diligent and continual reading of the

Hebrew Bible than by reading the Rabbinic commentaries, in which, as Förster writes in the preface of his lexicon, "There is no law, no knowledge of God, no Spirit, no true and dependable understanding of any discipline or art, no knowledge of any languages—no, not even of the Hebrew tongue." What is said here against the preposterous admirers of the Rabbis should be taken in a reasonable sense, lest one should conclude that all study applied to the Rabbinic commentaries and put to salutary use is simply condemned. Let the other tools for learning this language be sought by its regular professors.

CHAPTER 3.

THE STUDY OF CHALDAIC AND SYRIAC.

After the future Theologian has aspired to such knowledge of Hebrew that he more or less understands the Biblical text in the historical books, the study of Chaldaic and Syriac should be added, which is simply a matter of learning how the peculiar idioms of Hebrew differ from them in variations of terminations and in a few root words. (The same language is called *of the Chaldeans, Syriac, Babylonian, Assyrian, Chaldaic.* It is distinguished from Hebrew by characters, verb conjugations, pointing, vowel sound, idioms and several sayings of its own.) Knowledge of Chaldaic is necessary:

(1) on account of certain pericopes prescribed in Chaldaic or Syriac in the Old Testament. (There are six dialects of Aramaic or Syriac: (i) *The Babylonian* is the purest of all. It was used among the nobles and philosophers of Babylon. Daniel and Ezra wrote some things in this dialect. (ii) *The Chaldaic*, which was used in early paraphrases of the Bible by Onkelos, Jonathan, and R. Joseph. (iii) *The Jerusalem*, in which were written the later paraphrases on the law and the book of Esther. (iv) *The Median*, between the second and third Chaldaic Jerusalem, in which were written paraphrases on the Psalms, Proverbs, Job, Ecclesiastes, and Song of Solomon. (v) *The Talmudic*, which is a mixture, not only of the dialects mentioned above,

but also of many words taken from Hebrew, Latin, Greek, Arabic, and other foreign languages. (vi) The *Syro-Antiochene* or *Comagena*, which is also called *Maronitic* and is used by the Mesopotamians in their sacred writings.) The Hebrew Bible is divided by the Jews into *the Law, the Prophets, and the Sacred Writings*. Among these parts, there is none in which—for the sake of honor, as the Rabbis like to think (see R. Samuel ben Nahman in his larger exposition on Genesis)—God did not choose to use the Chaldaic language. In the Law, the "heap of stones," which Jacob the Hebrew and Laban the Syrian piled up as they entered into a covenant, was named by Laban in his own language. In the Prophets, an example is given of a letter which Jeremiah wrote in Chaldaic to the Jews who remained in Babylonia (Jer. 10). In the Sacred Writings, we find several chapters of Daniel and Ezra written in Chaldaic, containing a number of conversations and letters of the Chaldeans (Dan. 2:3–7; Ezra 4–7).

(2) On account of the Chaldaic paraphrases of the Old Testament. For since the Jewish people who spoke the genuine Hebrew tongue (whose integrity was preserved only in the sacred books and among the learned in the schools) were nearly obliterated after the Babylonian captivity and, in their daily speech, used the Chaldaic language which was imported into Palestine from Babylon, it was necessary to render the Hebrew Bible in the Chaldaic language for the sake of the common people of Judea. (See the treatise of Dr. Helvicus concerning the Chaldaic paraphrases.) It should be noted here that there is a threefold Targum: *the Babylonian, the Onkelos, and the Jerusalem.* Jonathan ben Uzziel, a disciple of Hillel and Simeon Justus (who held the infant Christ in his arms), a fellow disciple a hundred years before the destruction of the second temple

(that is, roughly 42 years before the birth of Christ), translated the Old Testament into Chaldaic. Galatinus writes this about his translation (lib. 1. *dearcanis Catholicae veritatis* cap. 3.): "He translated the sense from the sense, and thus he explained some very obscure phrases so that the things that had been written about the Messiah in a doubtful or hidden way he rendered certain and clear, to such an extent that his translation seems to be more of a commentary and exposition than an interpretation." Paul Weidner, a converted Jew, says this about Jonathan, from the book *Bava Bathara* (in *praefat. locorum fid. Christ.* p. 18.): "When he was not working on that translation, if a fly or any insect landed on him or on the paper, it would be immediately incinerated with fire from heaven without any harm to him or to the paper." Jonathan's translation is called the Babylonian Targum. Onkelus (or, as Galatinus calls him, Ankelos) came along almost a hundred years later, the disciple of the great R. Eleazar, nephew of Emperor Titus by his sister, who wrote his paraphrase after the destruction of the second temple. Some say that neither Jonathan nor Onkelos translated the whole Bible into the Chaldaic, but that Onkelos translated the Pentateuch, Jonathan the Prophets, while some also attribute the translation of the Psalter to R. Akila and R. Joseph the Blind (in Schindler's lexicon, on the word רגם): "Onkelos translated the five books of Moses, Jonathan the Prophets, R. Joseph the Sacred Writings, along with others." R. Akila follows Schindler (*Helvic. in tract. de paraph. Chald.* c. 2.), where he adds: "The third paraphrase of R. Joseph did not explain all the books of the Sacred Writings." For no Targum of Chronicles ever appeared, nor of Daniel, nor of Ezra, perhaps because most of the Chronicles had been explained in the books of the Kings, while large parts of Daniel and Ezra were already written in Chaldaic, so that there seemed to be no need of a new paraphrase. But Paul Fagius (in *praefat. Chald. paraph. a se editae*) testifies that both Onkelos and Jonathan had put together a complete translation of the Hebrew Bible, although nothing remains today of Onkelos' translation, except for a pericope on the Pentateuch. Galatinus testifies (in his work already cited) that he had seen Jonathan's translation of the Pentateuch, and that Jonathan's edition of the Psalter was still in existence, but they remained in the hands of only a few men so that they might keep it hidden away on account of the mysteries of the Christian faith that it contains. The Jerusalem Targum, which came after the earlier ones, differs from them significantly, but only in the chief passages of the Law. (The Targum Onkelos renders the Hebrew text literally, very close to the Hebrew word, and can therefore be understood very easily. But the Targum of Job and the Psalter is more obscure and more difficult. The Targum Onkelos is straightforward and literal, but the Targum Jonathan is freer, like the Targum Jerusalem, more of a commentary than a paraphrase.) But it is useful to compare the Chaldaic paraphrase with the Hebrew text, both on account of the authority that it has among the Jews—which is so great that, not only does no one dare to contradict it, but, as another testimony to its reliability, everyone everywhere uses it as the text itself, and therefore, whenever they find anything in the text of the Holy Bible to be ambiguous or difficult to understand, they always go back to this translation—and on account of the clarity of exposition it offers in several passages, from which the Jews may well be able to be convinced about Christ. For wherever it deals with Christ in the Hebrew verity by His proper name, there the name "Messiah" is almost always expressly used in the Chaldaic paraphrase, prompting Lyranus to write on Isaiah chapter 8: "The Chaldaic translation is declarative of the Hebrew verity in obscure passages." Nevertheless, discretion must be employed in the reading of the Chaldaic paraphrase, because Jewish fables and corruptions are sometimes found in it. It is somewhat purer in the Pentateuch, but even there it has it flaws. Thirdly, on account of certain Chaldaic and Syriac words in the New Testament which occur in the writings themselves of the Evangelists and Apostles, such as, *Ephphatha, Talitha, cumi, Maranatha*, etc. Angelo Canini diligently put together and explained those references, inquiring about the obscure passages in the New Testament, and from the use of these words he demonstrates that the Chaldaic language was the vernacular for Christ and the Apostles. (It is called 'Hebrew' by John and Luke because it was the vernacular at that time for the Hebrews.) Finally, on account of the *Pirushim*, the rabbinical commentaries, which are largely composed in Chaldaic and Syriac. The reading of these cannot be wholly neglected by the one who is to engage in arguments with the Jews. A knowledge of Syriac is useful on account of the Syriac paraphrase of the New Testament, which includes every book except for Second Peter, Second and Third John, Jude and Revelation. The Syrian language is of two kinds. One has its own characters for the letters of the alphabet, while the other uses the common Hebrew characters. The former is closely related in form to Arabic, although it has 28 letters. Widmannstadt's Syriac New Testament was also written in this form. The Syrian language which has its forms and letters in common with the Hebrews is either *Assyrian* or *Talmudic*. Assyrian is the language that the Jews in captivity had learned from their interaction with the Assyrians. And it is either *Chaldaic* or *Paraphrastic*. Chaldaic, which is also called Babylonian and Mesopotamian, is the dialect used by Laban the Syrian, Jeremiah, Daniel, and Ezra. Paraphrastic is the dialect used by the Chaldean translators in explaining the Hebrew Bible. Talmudic was used by the Talmudists in writing the Talmud after the paraphrases. There is a Babylonian Talmud, which is written in a purer style, and a Jerusalem Talmud, which is less pure. The rabbinic language that is used by our Jews today is related to the Talmudic. Tremellius draws this conclusion about it (in *praef. Syriacae paraph.*): "The Syriac, if perhaps not entirely, was yet mostly and most certainly derived from a Greek origin, but by which author or authors, or at what time—since it never occurred to us until now to inquire—nothing more can be determined at the present time except that the Greek and the Old Latin of the Old Testament are surely to be ascribed to those authors. Meanwhile, it is entirely consistent with the truth that the Syriac translation was made at the very beginning of the Church of Christ, either by the Apostles themselves or by their disciples, unless perhaps we prefer to imagine that they wanted to take only foreigners into account in their writing, while thinking either nothing or certainly very little of their own countrymen." The Syrians ascribe the origin of this translation of theirs to the Evangelist Mark. Alstedius (lib. 2. *praecogn.* cap. 113.) thinks it should be ascribed to the Antiochene Church and the Christians there. But its origin can hardly be attributed to the Apostles or to the time of the Apostles. (1) Because no direct mention of it exists among Clement of Alexandria, Origen, Eusebius, Athanasius, Theophilus, Epiphanius, Jerome, Cyril, Theodoret and others, who taught either in Syria or in Egypt, or who discussed the various editions of the Scriptures. (2) Because in the titles and chapter headings mention is made of the veneration of the cross, of prayers for the dead, of vigils, the commemoration of saints, and of other things of this kind which had not yet been brought into the Church at the time of the Apostles. Vergerius (Dial. 3. *contra Hosium*) recalls that he had asked Moses Meridinaeus whom he thought to have written the New Testament in the Syrian language. He replied that he did not know the author, that the manuscript was quite ancient and did not dissent from the Greek and Latin manuscripts. Vergerius claims to have heard from this same Moses that Widmannstadt, in addition to a Gospel written in Syriac, also had several other pages written in Syriac, but Moses himself admitted that these were not many years old; that in them was an index of the kind that the papists are wont to affix to their editions of the New Testament, and a certain fragment that is to be read on the day of the dedication of the temple, etc. Rutgerus Speius (in *praefat. Gramm. Arab.*) testifies that the Heidelberg manuscript was written 800 years ago. Junius comments that there is a very old Syriac manuscript in the Heidelberg library in which there are notes concerning festivals, written in the margin by a more recent hand, and mention is made of Antonius Monachus and of others who are several ages removed from the time of the Apostles. Albert Widmannstadt, chancellor of Emperor Ferdinand, was the first in Europe to oversee the printing of a Syriac New Testament in Vienna in 1556. Since the Antiochene Patriarch used Syriac in his churches (where it was understood), and not Latin, and since he lacked the necessary instruments, that is, books for ministry, he sent a certain clergyman named Moses Meridinaeus to oversee the printing of the New Testament in Syriac either in Rome or in Venice. But since this happened in vain, he turned to Emperor Ferdinand and fell in with the most learned Albert Widmannstadt, who took great delight in the same kind of literature. He himself had been contemplating an edition of the Syrian New Testament. Thus, after the matter was related to the emperor, at his command Widmannstadt not only oversaw the printing, but also took up, together with Moses, the work of correcting it. In 1568,

Tremellius' Syriac Testament appeared, printed with Hebrew characters. He is said to have used not only Widmannstadt's edition, but also another more ancient codex, the manuscript from the Heidelberg library. In the royal Bibles also there is a Latin translation of the Syriac New Testament, prepared by that great scholar Guido Fabricius. But for the one who desires to learn these languages, the following may prove useful: The tables of Johann Mercer in *Linguae Chaldaeae Grammaticen*, edited by Schindler in 1579; Tremellius' *Grammatica Chaldaea et Syra*, which is found underneath the Syriac Testament; *Grammatica et Lexicon Syriacum* of Crinesius; but especially Schindler's *Lexicon Pentaglottum*. (Just as Chaldaic and Syriac have their origin from the Hebrew language, Arabic comes from these two, which was once in use among the Saracens and is now the vernacular throughout all Asia and Africa. The Psalter exists in Arabic produced by Augustine, Bishop of Nebbio, but it is poorly printed. Clenard. (in *fine libr. 1. Epistl.*) and Guido Fabricius (in *praefat. Nov. Test. Syriaci p. ult.*) prove that all the sacred writings exist in Arabic. The Arabs are said to have several epistles of Paul edited in no language. The Arabic New Testament was printed in Rome in 1592, etc.)

CHAPTER 4.

THE STUDY OF GREEK.

There are three reasons why the knowledge of Greek is necessary for the future Theologian:

(1) On account of the Greek text of the New Testament, which alone is authentic. Some of the Fathers, such as Origen, Eusebius, Jerome and others, think that the Gospel history of Matthew was written in Hebrew. (Münster and Tilius oversaw the public printing of the Hebrew Gospel of Matthew, but it is spurious, containing serious errors in the Hebrew itself.) Guido Fabricius suspects the same concerning the Epistle to the Hebrews, that it was written in Hebrew. Baronius (*tom. 1. annal. anno 45.*) tries to prove (*ex Pontificali Damasci in vita Petri*) that Mark's Gospel was written in Latin, but Bellarmine does not support his opinion (*libr. 2. de verbo Dei cap. 7.*) But it is more correctly stated that each and every book of the New Testament was written by the Evangelists and Apostles in Greek, which was not only familiar at that time to the Gentiles, but also to the vast majority of Jews who lived in Asia Minor. Therefore, only the Greek text is original and authentic, and thus even those who imagine that some books of the New Testament were written in some other language attribute the translation of them into Greek to the Apostles as the authors. For Athanasius, in his synopsis, thinks that the

Gospel of Matthew was translated into Greek by the Apostle James. Theophylact attributes that translation to the Apostle John, while some ascribe it to Mark and others to Matthew himself. Clement of Alexandria states that the Epistle to the Hebrews, written by Paul in Hebrew, was converted to Greek by Luke, but Eusebius (lib. 3. *history*. cap. 34.) more correctly attributes that idea to Clement of Rome. They say the same thing about Mark. They foolishly claim, without any support from antiquity, that Mark first wrote in Latin, and that he himself translated his own Gospel into Greek in Aquileia. It remains, therefore, that the Greek text in the New Testament is authentic and consequently that the knowledge of Greek is necessary in order to consult the sources* in the New Testament. (Bellarmine [lib. 2. *de verbo Dei*. cap. 7.] tries to prove that the Greek sources are not everywhere uncorrupted, and that it is not always safe to correct the Latin with the Greek. But his arguments are unfounded.)

(2) On account of the Greek translation of the Old Testament, which is customarily known by the name of its LXX translators. There were once various Greek editions, as one gathers from the ecclesiastical writers (Eusebius [lib. 6. *Hist*. cap. 13.], Athanasius [in *synopsi*.], and Epiphanius [*de mensura et ponderibus*] list the translations in order.) Clement of Alexandria (libr. 1. *stromat*.) mentions a certain Greek version of uncertain authorship that appeared before the monarchy was handed over to the Greeks. Plato and the more ancient philosophers were said to have drawn many things from this version, but it fell out of use as it was succeeded by that famous translation of the Seventy. Thus the version known as that of the LXX translators is the second translation, to which most

---

*   *fontes*

of the Fathers appeal. Augustine (lib. 18. *de C. D. c.* 43.): "Although there were also other interpreters who translated the sacred utterances from Hebrew into Greek, such as Aquila, Symmachus, Theodotion, such as also that translation whose author's name is not given and is therefore known as the anonymous fifth edition, nevertheless the Church receives this version of the LXX as if it were the only version, and the Greek Christians use it as well, most of whom are unaware that any other exists." Justin reviews the occasion for this translation (*apol. 2. pro Christianis* pag. 56.): "When the Ptolemaic King of the Egyptians* established the library by the decree of Strabo Lamsacenus and sought to collect the writings of all men, he sent to Herod, King of the Jews**, to be informed about the Prophets among the Jews, asking that a copy of the Prophetic books be made for him. King Herod complied, ordering that those writings be sent to him in the Hebrew language. But since the Egyptians did not understand the things that were written, he again sent a delegation and asked him to send men to him that they might translate those books into Greek. So it

---

*   Irenaeus (lib. 3. c. 25.) and Clement of Alexandria (lib. 1. *Strom.*) call him "Ptolemy the son of Lagus," but Aristaeus (in *historia de hac re*), Josephus (lib. 12. *antiq.* cap. 2.), Philo (lib. 2. *de vita Mosis.*), Tertullian (in *Apol.* cap. 48.), Epiphanius (*de mensur. et ponder.*), and Augustine (18. *de civ. Dei* cap. 42.) state more correctly that it was done by *Ptolemy Philadelphus* in the 17th year of the kingdom, which was 291 years before the birth of Christ. Junius thinks it was established by Ptolemy the son of Lagus and completed by Philadelphus.

**   A truer account is that of Augustine, that he sent instead to Eleazar the High Priest (lib. 18. *de civ. Dei* cap. 42.): "He sent royal gifts into the temple of God and asked that the Scriptures then be given to him by the High Priest Eleazar." At the time of Josephus (lib. 12. *autiq.* cap. 2.) the letters of Ptolemy to the High Priest Eleazar and of Eleazar to the king are still extant.

was done, and the books have remained among the Egyptians to this day." Other writers add that seventy-two elders were sent, namely, six from every tribe of the children of Israel, men who were very skillful in Greek and Hebrew, (Possevinus [in *apparatu suo sacro* tom. 3. pag. 205.] lists the names of the seventy-two translators.) who, at Pharus of Egypt, in the space of seventy-two days, translated the divine words from Hebrew into Greek with miraculous consensus. (Aristaeus, who wrote a history of that famous translation, says that he was an attendant of Ptolemy, but Ludovicus Vives [in lib. 18. *de civ. Dei* cap. 42.] thinks that the book of Aristaeus was concocted by a more someone more recent.) Before Jerome translated the Bible from Hebrew into Latin, the LXX boasted the highest authority in the Church. Augustine (lib. 15. *de civ. Dei* cap. 23.): "The LXX translators are rightly believed to have received the Prophetic Spirit, so that, if they changed anything by His authority and uttered anything that they were interpreting differently than it was, there was no doubt that it had been divinely uttered." See also Augustine (lib. 18. *de C.D.* c. 42.): "Ptolemy, wanting to put them (the elders) to the test, and fearing that they would perhaps agree to hide the truth that was in the Scriptures through their translation, separated them from one another and ordered them all to interpret the same Scripture. This he did for all the books. But when they came together as one in front of Ptolemy and compared their translations, God was glorified, and the Scriptures were believed to be truly divine, as the elders all recited the same translation, with both the same verbs and the same nouns, from beginning to end, so that even the Gentiles of the present day might know that the Scriptures were translated through the inspiration[*] of God." See Irenaeus (lib. 3. c. 25. pag. 116.): "Peter and John and Matthew and Paul

---

[*]   *aspirationem*

and then the rest and their followers announced all the Prophetic things just as the translation of the elders contains them. For one and the same Spirit of God, who heralded in the Prophets the advent of the Lord and what kind of advent it would be—this Spirit interpreted well through the elders the things that had been well prophesied. He Himself also announced in the Apostles that the fullness of the times of adoption had come." Irenaeus follows Justin in this matter, who likewise asserts (in *orat. exhortat. ad gentes*) that "each one of them was secluded in his own private cell, and the entire Scripture was translated by each one with the very same words." (Josephus and Philo think that only the Law of Moses was translated by the LXX interpreters. But (i) Ptolemy would not have been content with only a translation of the Pentateuch; he wanted his new library to be as complete as possible. (ii) There would have been no miracle in the swiftness of this translation being completed over the span of seventy-two days. (iii) The Apostles used the Greek version in citing the testimonies of the Prophets. But at that time no other version existed except for that of the LXX translators.) In fact, he adds that he himself had seen traces of those cells in Alexandria. Cyril (*Catec.* 4.), Clement of Alexandria (lib. 3. *stromat.*) and others concur with Justin and Irenaeus. But Epiphanius (*l. de mensur. et pond.*) writes that "these translators were secluded two by two in each cell," for which reason, no matter how excellent they make that translation, nevertheless Augustine (lib. 2. *de doctrine. Christ.* capit. 15.) does not dare to confirm with certainty the assertion about the cells. Jerome (in *praefat. Pentateuch.*) is more confident: "I do not know which author first constructed the seventy cells of Alexandria with his lies, since neither Aristaeus, who took part in the matter, nor Josephus, in telling the story, make any mention of those cells. It is one thing to be a prophet, another to be a translator." Here some make reference to that version whose production Herod oversaw at the demand of the last Ptolemy (who was the younger brother of Cleopatra). Justin says (*apol.* 2.) that some want to equate this version with the one the Father used to refer to with the singular name κοινήν, *the common version*, and which, afterward, Lucian restored in emended form, wherefore it is also referred to by many as the *Lucianic* version. Orosius describes the occasion for this version (lib. 6. cap. 14.) The third translation of the Old Testament into Greek was done in the twelfth year of Emperor Hadrian, 138 years after the birth of Christ, by Aquila Ponticus, who was first converted to the Christian faith from Paganism, but afterward relapsed into Judaism, at which time he also translated the Scriptures, which is why his is not considered a translation made in good faith. (He was cast out of the Church on account of his excessive study of judicial astrology. He was a disciple of R. Akiva.) The fourth translation was done by Theodotion Ephesius (Ponticus is to Epiphanius what Ephesius is to Euthymius), who became a proselyte of the Jews after being a Marcionite heretic. He prepared his version during the reign of Commodus in the year 184. Epiphanius (*lib. de mensural ac ponder.*) pays him this tribute: that he translated the Hebrew Scriptures with greater faith than others. But Theodoret says that he translated them with a perverse spirit and in bad faith. The fifth translation belongs to Symmachus the Samaritan (among the seven Wise Men of Samaria), who undertook his translation in the year 203, during the time of Emperor Severus. He was at first an Ebionite, but then gave himself over to Judaism after receiving a second circumcision. The sixth translation is anonymous. It was found inside large earthenware vessels in Nicopolis during the thirtieth year of the reign of Alexander, son of Mammaea. From all these editions (except the first) Origen put together what was called the Hexapla, or the Tetrapla, or even the Octopla. (An assistant of a certain good and wealthy man named Ambrose, Adamantius was also called Chalcenterus on account of his continual labors.)[*] For he first divided each page into six columns. Then he wrote in the first column the Hebrew text with Hebrew letters. In the second, he wrote the same text with Greek letters. In the third, he included Aquila's translation. In the fourth, the translation of Symmachus. In the fifth, the translation of Theodotion. These volumes were called the Tetrapla on account of the four translators, the Hexapla on account of the six columns. He then added those two translations of uncertain authorship in two other columns and called those volumes the Octopla. He indicated the different Scriptures with adjacent ribbons. As for the LXX translation itself, which had been received and approved for common use, he arranged it in such a way that, from it alone, in a single glance, one could easily determine what was in the Hebrew text and what was not. For since those translators often added many things of their own for the sake of explaining the things that were being treated and just as often deliberately omitted many things which they thought to be redundant, and since he considered anything beyond that what was contained in the Hebrew text to have been added, he butchered, as it were, the things that were added by adding critical markings[**] of his own. And where things had been removed, he substituted the translation of Theodotion and noted it with asterisks. One certain wishes that the Hexapla of Origen still survived to the present day, but they perished by

---

[*] Epiphanius (*haeres. 63. ac lib. de mens. ac. ponderib.*), Possevinus (*in apparatu sacro ex Sixto Senensi tom. 3. p. 234.*), Eusebius (*lib. 6. Histor. capit. 13.*)

[**] *obeliscis*

the injury of time. The eighth edition belongs to Origen, who emended the translation of the LXX with many phrases from Theodotion mixed in and marked with a star, and with many words crossed out with an obelus or with a spit, so that he seemed to have made a new edition which was called κοινή, Koiné, because of its daily use in the Church. The ninth translation of the Old Testament was made by Lucian the Elder and Martyr. It was found in Nicomedia in a certain wall, preserved within a marble arch. (Athanasius in *Synopsi*.) The tenth is of Hesychius, who again emended the LXX translation and passed it on to the Churches of Egypt. (Jerome in *praefat. in Paralip*.) (Some add the translation of Sophronus.) The translation that exists today is normally referred to as the LXX, but scholars have good reason to doubt whether it is the same translation made by the LXX translators. For Aristaeus, in his history of this translation, and Philo (lib. 2. *de vita Mosis*) testify that the LXX translators translated everything with the utmost fidelity and propriety, even word for word, and that their translation was examined diligently by many people before it was placed into the royal library, and that it was praised by all for its fidelity and propriety. But the Greek version which we now have dissents from the Hebrew in many places. It includes some things that are not in the Hebrew text, and it omits others that are, as Jerome demonstrates (*praef. in Pentateuch. in Ep. ad Suniam et alibi*). There also occur in it manifest errors, especially in the computation of years in Genesis 5 and in many other places. (Methuselah, according to the Greek translation, was still alive for fourteen years after the flood. But where was he kept during the flood? Augustine (lib. 15. *de civ. Dei* cap. 11.) twists himself in a knot trying to resolve this problem. Jonah 3 in the Greek says that Nineveh was to be destroyed in three days, but in Hebrew its destruction is more correctly set after 40 days, for Jonah could hardly travel through the city in three days.) But if even long ago the LXX began to be emended by Origen, Lucian, Hesychius, and Jerome, how, then, was it free from errors? And if it contracted corruptions within the first three hundred years, who should believe that it has remained uncorrupted during the past 1,300 years? Justin writes (in *Dialog. cum Tryphone* p. 231.): "Your teachers simply removed many entire passages of the Scriptures from the translation of those elders who were with Ptolemy, in which it is clearly shown that this very One who was crucified is God and Man, and that He was foretold to hang on a cross and die." He proves this in the same place with many examples. (Baronius thinks [*Casaub. exerc. 1.* cap. 34.] that the Greek edition of the Bible kept in Rome was the very same translation of the LXX. This opinion could hardly be excused in a novice of theological study, much less in a man of such great name!) Add to this that the Greek translation in many places cannot be reconciled in any way with the Hebrew text, unless the pointing is removed and the text is read differently than the pointing requires. The argument is that the author of that translation used a Bible that was not pointed, which cannot be said about the LXX translators. We conclude, therefore, that the Greek version which we use today is plainly a translation that is either different than that pristine version of the LXX translators (as Drusius [lib. 6. *observant.* cap. 9] and Whitaker [*de script.* q. 2. capit. 3.] state), or, if it is the same (as some are persuaded from the testimonies that are cited from the Fathers from the LXX and are also found in our Greek manuscripts), nevertheless it is so corrupted and damaged that it should with good reason be called and considered to be something else. Andreas Osiander (lib. 1. *annot. in Harmoniam Evang.* c. 10.) employs another argument to prove this same thing. "The Seventy only translated Moses. Therefore the Greek edition of the Prophets which we now have does not belong to the LXX." He deduces this from Philo (*lib. de vita Mosis*) and from Jerome (in *qq. Hebraicis et in c. 5. Ezech.*). In this Pagnini agrees with him. But Justin (in *Dial. cum Tryphone*), Irenaeus (l. 3. c. 25.), Clement of Alexandria (lib. 1. *Stromat.*) and many others state more correctly that all the books of the Old Testament were translated by the LXX, for why would the king who was trying so zealously to bring all the collected books of the whole world into the Alexandrian library have sought only the translation of the Law of Moses and not also of the Prophets? Add to this that there would have been no miracle in the swiftness of the translation if only the Pentateuch had been translated over the span of 72 days. Theodoret says that the Jews did not only send to Ptolemy a portion of the Scriptures, but the whole Scripture, written with golden letters.

(3) On account of the reading of the Greek Fathers: Justin, Athanasius, Chrysostom, Nazianzus, Epiphanius, Isodorus, Pelusiota, Damascene, etc.), of which more will be said later on. Some very useful tools for acquiring a knowledge of Greek are discussed elsewhere. The reading of Xenophon, Demosthenes, Plutarch, the Suida, etc., will help the student become acquainted with the properties of words and phrases. But above all, Henry Stephanus' *Thesaurus*, which is truly a treasury of Greek scholarship, and the Lexicon of Budaeus are highly commended to all students of this language.

SECTION 2: THE KNOWLEDGE OF PHILOSOPHY.

In Acts 17:18, the holy Apostle's dialogue with the Athenian philosophers is recorded. But as his reward for this dialogue, he was considered by them to be a σπερμόλογος, *a babbler*, and when he spoke in the court of the Areopagus about the resurrection of the dead, he was ridiculed and insulted by most of them. The Apostle undoubtedly had that day in mind when he later wrote to the Colossians from a Roman prison and gravely warned them that no one should seduce them with philosophy. His words of admonition are emphatic in Colossians 2:8: "Take heed that no one rob you through philosophy and empty deceit, according to the tradition of men, according to the basic principles of the world, and not according to Christ." The word βλέπετε, *take heed*, indicates that they have fallen down here, and therefore special care must be taken, just as Christ said when He commanded His disciples to watch out for the seductions of false prophets and false Christs. He says in Mat. 14:4: "Take heed that no one seduce you." Likewise, He carefully warns them to beware the false doctrine of the Pharisees as He says in Mark 8:15: "Beware of the yeast of the Pharisees." In Mark 13:5, 9, 23 and 33, He repeats this admonition four times and continually requires that special attention be paid. Συλαγωγεῖν, means *to pillage, to carry off some booty in war*, which is the privilege of conquerors. The word καταβραβεύεσθαι corresponds to this in v. 18, *to cheat out of reward or prizes.* Jerome (in qq. *ad Algasiam* q. 10.): "It is called καταβραβεύεσθαι when someone in a contest loses the prize and victory that is due him, either by the injustice of the superintendent of games or by the deceit of the magistrates." Others explain it in this way: "Let no one assume the role of Judge against you," speaking metaphorically of the superintendents of the public games who are called βραβεῦται. The sense of the Apostle's admonition, then, is that Christians should not entrust the judgment of the lofty mysteries of the faith to corrupt philosophy, lest they should be cheated out of the possession of the truth and lose the victory that has been set forth for them in the course of this life. As a matter of exegesis, he combines philosophy with κενῆς ἀπάτης, *empty deceit*, in order to show which philosophy he means, namely, that which does not contain itself within its own sphere and its own terms, but that cleverly devises such things by which it trusts that the truth of heavenly doctrine can be overturned, which are really inane spider webs on account of the axioms that have been wickedly applied. For this reason, he also adds that such philosophical dogmas are "according to the tradition of men, and according to the basic elements of the world, and not according to Christ." In other words, philosophy teaches human, not divine, doctrine. It deals with earthly things, not the heavenly mysteries. It has dogmas of human wisdom, but it teaches nothing about Christ, as Osiander rightly comments on this passage: "One can readily understand this 'human tradition' and 'the basic elements of the world' as the ancient practices drawn from traditions and the worship of the Law, so that the first part is a reference to the weapons of the Gentiles, while the second two refer to the weapons of the Jews, with which both Jews and Gentiles were attacking the Gospel." From this well of Apostolic admonition flowed the grievances and accusations of the Fathers—later proven correct by the very practice in the Church—with which they attacked the pagan philosophers of their time. Tertullian (*lib. adv. Hermog.* p. 339.) calls them the "Patriarchs of the heretics." Jerome praises this saying of Tertullian (in *Epist. ad. Ctesiphont.* tom. 3. f. 114.). He writes the same thing (lib. 1. *adv. Marcion* p. 154.), that "every heresy is given life from the devices of the philosophers." Origen (*hom. 4. ad 7. cap. Exod.*) understands the flies and frogs with which the Egyptians were stricken to be the vain chattering of the Dialectics and the arguments of the Sophists. Ambrose testifies (libr. 7. *de fide* capit. 3.) that "Arius established all the force of his venom through Dialectic disputation." That famous saying of Socrates agrees with this (libr. 2. *Histor. Eccles.* cap. 28.): "Aristotle led Aetius into the most shameful error of Arius." Basil (in c. 2. *Esai.*) calls the Dialectic *Bellatrix*, a female warrior. Nazianzus (in *orat. de modest. in disp. serv.*): "They have wickedly introduced into the Church the analyses of Chrysippus' syllogisms, the deceit of Aristotle's devices, and the spells of Plato's eloquence, like certain Egyptian plagues." Anselm (*de incarnatione ad Urbanum* cap. 2.): "Since all people should be strongly warned to approach questions of the sacred page with the greatest care, surely those Dialectics of our time—indeed, the dialectically heretical—should be summarily blown away from the discussion of spiritual questions." But all these and similar things must be understood, not concerning the true and salutary use of philosophy, but concerning the abuse of it; not about philosophy in the abstract, but concretely about the deceivers who abuse philosophy.

In order that one may be able to form a better judgment in this matter, we shall offer some instruction concerning both the use as well as the abuse of philosophy in theology. *The use is laudable; the abuse is criminal.*

CHAPTER 1.

THE MANIFOLD AND SALUTARY USE OF PHILOSOPHY IN THEOLOGY.

There is a threefold use of philosophy in theology: ὀργανικὸς (organic), κατασκευαστικὸς (confirming), and ἀνασκευαστικός (refuting). The organic use extends very broadly, but for the sake of instruction it can be reduced to certain definite headings which, for ease of understanding, should be presented by a division of the branches of philosophy. The branches of philosophy are either *instrumental* or *real*. The instrumental branches are Logic and Rhetoric. (Grammar contains the study of languages, which we have already treated.) The real branches are either *Theoretical*, such as Metaphysics, Physics, and Mathematics; or *Practical*, such as Ethics, Politics, and Economics.

(1) Concerning the branches of philosophy that are *universally studied*, both real and instrumental, we say in general that the knowledge of them excites, sharpens, prepares, and perfects a man's mind, so that he is able more quickly and with minimal work to advance in any study of the higher disciplines. It is this preparatory benefit that is also of service to the future theologian. Augustine (lib. 1. *de ordine.*): "A reasonably disciplined and succinct education in the liberal arts produces live-

lier and more persistent and more sophisticated men who are devoted to embracing the truth, so that they seek it more ardently and follow it more steadfastly and finally hold to it more delightfully." Origen (*homil. 14. in Genes.*, near the end): "If you are not still a child, if you do not require milk, if instead you bring to the table awakened senses and, having already received plentiful instruction, you approach more fit to understand the word of God, there is, indeed, a great banquet set for you." Pico Mirandola: "Human philosophy aids contemplation. Since it illuminates the intellect, it also indirectly removes the errors in which we are often entangled because of our ignorance, and it seems to inflame the mind and to move it from temporal and fleeting things to focus on the eternal, so that the sacred utterances may be more readily and more clearly grasped."

(2) We say specifically concerning the real branches of philosophy that the knowledge of them serves theology in the explanation of certain terms. Theology uses two kinds of terms. Some, which are called *Biblical terms*, are expressly used in the Scriptures; others, drawn from the Scriptures and the ecclesiastical teachers, express things that are understood in the Scriptures, even though the terms themselves are not used. These are called *Ecclesiastical terms*. In both cases, philosophy often contributes something to the more accurate explanation of the terms. Since the terms *Being, good, true, perfect, finite, infinite, person, existence, essence, act, power*, etc., are metaphysical terms, the knowledge of metaphysics can contribute something to the explanation of them. *Time, place, heaven, earth, sea, fire, snow, hail, rain, the faculties of the soul*, etc., are physical terms, so the theologians seeks an explanation of them from physics. The theologian is unable to speak about the journeys of the Patriarchs, of the Israelites in the wilderness, of the Apostles, etc.,

without a knowledge of geography. Likewise he is unable to speak about the course of the stars, about Orion and the Pleiades, without a knowledge of astronomy. For the one who is going to discuss virtues, temperance, generosity, valor, etc., political matters, the magistrate, subjects, laws, punishments, etc., economics, husband, wife, children, servants, etc., a knowledge of Practical Philosophy provides assistance. Jerome's words (in *praefat. lament. Jerem.*) apply here: "We are not capable of grasping those things in the Scriptures which are more important to know, unless we have received an introduction in them from ethics." Eusebius has Origen in mind when he writes (lib. 6. c. 18.) that "he also put the disciplines of philosophy and mathematics into the schools among the sacred subjects and urged students with particular diligence to acquire a knowledge of the liberal arts," affirming that "they are a necessary tool for explaining and for discussing the Holy Scriptures."

But as we have noted, philosophy serves theology in the explanation of *some* terms, for there are some terms, such as *Christ, Holy Spirit, election, etc.,* that are purely theological, in which case philosophy contributes nothing at all to their explanation. And as we have also noted, philosophy *serves* in the explanation of terms. Therefore, we also ascribe to it in this area, not a *mastery*, but a *ministry**. Consequently, no matter how much a term may pertain to philosophy, nevertheless, the theologian is not allowed to explain or apply it any differently, nor to free it from every imperfection, to the point that philosophy should contribute anything to its explanation alongside the proper principle of his knowledge; namely, that the Scripture interprets the term. For since the Father is said in divine

---

*　　*non magisterium, sed ministerium*

matters to be the *beginning*,* and the term 'beginning' is a philosophical term, nevertheless, it does not follow that the conditions which are applied to the term 'beginning' in Metaphysics
should all be attributed at once to the Father, but theology uses
the term with a certain law of its own and with a sound explanation already added. *Generation* is a term of physics. But when
the Father is said in divine matters to generate the Son, it should
by no means be inferred that all those conditions of generation
taught by physics are to be brought in here. *Righteousness* is a term
of ethics. But one should not turn to the rules of ethics to draw
the conclusion that the one who does righteous things is righteous
before God. Instead, he should draw his conclusion from the Holy
Scriptures, which teach that righteousness is by faith, etc. Luther
(in *libro de votis Monasticis* cap. 3.): "The impure and obscene harlot
of the Parisian school has determined that Aristotle's dogmas do
not dissent in morals from the dogmas of Christ, since he does not
teach anything other than that virtues are acquired through works.
He says, 'We are made temperate by doing temperate things'—
which the Christian conscience despises as hellish bilge water
and says, 'By believing in Christ, who is temperate, I, too, shall
be made temperate; His temperance is mine as a gift.'"

Therefore, the safest thing is to attend singularly and
chiefly to the nomenclature of the Holy Spirit and only afterwards, for the sake of comparison, to bring in the philosophical
explanation of the terms. Chemnitz (part. 1. *Locor. Theologicor.
de creation.* cap. 3.): "It cannot be factually denied, nor should it
be falsely discredited, that, if the doctrines (the heavenly and
the philosophical) are compared in a legitimate way and each is
confined within its own boundaries, the true and proper doctrine of the Church is usefully illustrated."

---

* *principium*

(3) One must treat the *instrumental* branches of philosophy distinctly. Logic serves theology by teaching the laws of definitions, division, method, and arguments, so that the theologian can present theological matters distinctly and in an orderly way, explain controversial questions more clearly, shape them more plainly, and refute his adversaries more convincingly. To this pertain those warm praises which the Fathers attribute to logic. Clement of Alexandria (*1. Strom.*): "Philosophy is found to be a coworker and assistant of the (heavenly) truth. As the first and second step to him who goes up into the attic, so is grammar to the one who is about to philosophize. For clarity brings with it the ability to teach truth and doctrine, lest we be overthrown by heresies. Indeed, it is, in itself, a perfect doctrine of the Savior and lacking in nothing, since it is the power and wisdom of God. Philosophy, moreover, as it approaches, does not make the truth more powerful, but instead weakens the Sophistical argumentation against it as it wards off the cunning traps set against the truth, like a shelter and a fence and a wall." Augustine (libr. 2. *de ordine* cap. 2.): "Dialectic is the discipline of disciplines. It teaches both to teach and to learn, to know what one knows and to cause others to know." He further professes (lib. 3. *contra Academic.* cap. 13.) that "this great art had provided him assistance in refuting the sophistical arguments of the heretics." (libr. 2. *de doctrina Christiana* cap. 31.) "The discipline of debate is most beneficial for all kinds of questions in the Sacred Writings that must be penetrated and refuted." (lib. 1. *contra Crescon.* cap. 20.): "Christian doctrine does not fear this art which they call 'Dialectic,' which does nothing other than to demonstrate logical consequences, namely, true things by means of true things, false by means of false, just as the Apostle did not fear it in the Stoics, whom he did not refuse when they wanted to confer with him." Basil (in

cap. 5. *Esaiae*): "The true virtue of Dialectic is that it distinctly divides the natures of things that are related to one another. It distinguishes the things that are related to one another and it discerns the things that are contrary." Nazianzus (in *Epistol. ad 150. Episcop.*): "The old truth is brought to light by means of logical disputations."

Rhetoric serves theology by teaching the precepts of eloquence, with explanations of figures and tropes, etc. Consequently, the study of it is not to be considered unimportant for the future theologian, as we read (dist. 37.): "It is read that the Lord commanded Israel to despoil the Egyptians of their gold and silver, which instructs us morally that, whether it be the gold of wisdom or the silver of eloquence that we find among the Poets, we should convert it to the use of salutary education. In Leviticus, moreover, we are ordered to offer the Lord the firstfruits of honey, that is, of human eloquence."

The confirming use consists in the confirmation of questions. Moreover, there are two kinds of questions in theology. Some concern the lofty mysteries of the faith which have been set beyond all the grasp of human reason, such as the mystery of the Trinity, the incarnation, the resurrection, etc. But some have been set up in such a way that the human intellect is able to rise up to some knowledge of them through common goodwill and through the discourse that is derived from an inspection of creation, for example, that God exists, that He is good, just, and a punisher of crimes. (The former are properly said to be πιστά – reliable, the latter are said to be ἐπιστητά – knowable. The things that can be learned about God naturally, insofar as they are not properly articles of faith, since the articles of faith are not known by nature, cannot be gathered by signs from nature, but are either divinely revealed principles or conclusions deduced from them.) Questions of the first kind cannot be proven and confirmed by philosophical arguments, for philosophy cannot contribute and confirm from its own principles that which it plainly does not know. The words of Ambrose apply here (libr. 1. *de fide* cap. 5.): "Remove the arguments where faith is demanded, etc." Augustine (exempla 3. *ad Volus.*): "If reason is demanded, it is not miraculous. If an example is sought, it is not remarkable." Thomas (part. 1. quaest. 32. art. 1.): "He who depends on reason to prove the Trinity detracts from faith in two ways, first, because it is the dignity of faith to concern itself with the invisible things that go beyond human reason. And he detracts from faith, secondly, with respect to the utility of drawing others to it. For unbelievers believe that we depend on reasons of this kind, although they are not compelling. Therefore, one should not attempt to prove matters of faith except by the authorities." Yet nothing prohibits one, for the sake of any illustration whatsoever, from explaining those mysteries with some parallels sought from the book of Nature. But it must be done cautiously, sparingly, having also demonstrated at the same time the manner of dissimilarity. Nor can it be rejected altogether if some things are adduced for the purpose of convincing the Gentiles from the books of the Gentiles in explaining these mysteries—not that one should conclude that they were able to aspire to the knowledge of those things by the light of Nature, but that they perceived such things, either by reading the divine oracles, or by conversing with the people of Israel, or by the fame of the Prophetic proclamation; as the Fathers say, they stole from the people of God.

Philosophical arguments can also be brought in for the purpose of confirming questions of the second kind, not out of necessity, as if theology were unable sufficiently to confirm them from its own principles, but out of abundance, that it may be plainly evident that not only the light of grace, but also the light of Nature reaches out to answer them in a certain way—not in a primary way, as if the force of proof consisted primarily in those philosophical arguments, but in a secondary and less important way. Here belongs the statement of Scaliger (exerc. 6. sect. 3.): "An artist takes questions, propositions, and conclusions from an artist in two ways: in one way, when the knowledge of the inferior depends entirely on the principles of the superior, which happens in the lower sciences; in the other way, when the artist admits those things which have been posited by another, which he also learned without him, but not as principles of his own, nor as things proved by another, as if he himself could not prove it, but in order to examine and judge them." In the second way, not the first, a theologian takes some things from philosophy. Thomas, with this in view, distinguishes between preceding and following reasons. Origen (homil. 14. in Genes. tom. 1. p. 46.): "Philosophy is neither contrary to, nor in harmony with, the Law of God in all things. For many of the philosophers write that there is one God who created all things. In this, they agree with the Law of God. Some have also added that God both made and rules all things through His Word, and that the Word is God, by whom all things are governed. In this, they not only write in agreement with the Law, but also with the Gospels. Indeed, morals and physics, which is called philosophy, perceive practically all things that belong to us. But they dissent from us when they say that matter is coeternal with God. They dissent when they deny that God oversees mortal affairs, but claim instead that His providence is restrained above the lunar sphere. They dissent from us when they weigh the lives of those who are born based on the courses of the stars. They dissent when they say that this world is eternal and is never to have an end. But there are also many other things in which they either disagree or are in harmony with us." To the class of these latter questions also belong those things which are transferred from philosophy to theology; namely, concerning the origin of the soul, the communication of character, location, whether the quality of the body is essential, etc. In the discussion of these and similar questions, arguments can be sought from the principles of philosophy, but only in such a way that they are subordinated to theological reasons.

The refuting use consists in attacking and refuting questions, which one should consider in the following way. False and erroneous doctrines are first to be refuted from the proper principle of theology, namely, from the Holy Scripture, which is the proper, chief, and effective thing that refutes. Afterwards the reasons of philosophy can also be added, so that one may be shown not only how to fight the false doctrine with the light of grace, but also with the light of Nature, which is the secondary proof, less important, and plainly ineffective apart from the first. Luther (in *libro de votis Monasticis* capit. 5.): "Nature, although in itself it does not arrive at the light and works of God, so that in affirmatives (as they say) its judgment is false, nevertheless, in negatives it is true. For reason does not grasp what is God, and yet it most certainly grasps what is not God. Thus, although it does not see what is right and good before God (namely, faith), it plainly knows unbelief, that murder is evil. Christ also uses reason when He says that every kingdom divided against itself is deserted. Paul uses it when he says that Nature also does not teach that a woman should prophesy with a bare head. Therefore, whatever is clearly opposed to this reason is certainly also much more opposed to God, for how will that which opposes earthly truth not oppose the heavenly truth?" This statement of Luther should be understood concerning those theological questions to which the light of Nature can extend and in which it is consistent with the light of grace. But when, in the lofty mysteries of faith, the truth of a certain doctrine has been demonstrated from the immovable foundations of Scripture, no philosophical reasons are to be set against it, and if they are, they should not be heard. Augustine (Epistola 7. *ad Marcellin.*, near the middle): "If reason is rendered contrary to the authority of the divine Scriptures, no matter how sharp it may be, it lacks in true conformity, for it cannot be true."

To the refuting use of philosophy also pertains the fact that the arguments of the adversaries can be overturned by means of the earnestness sought from Nature itself. Thus, when the Arians say that "that which is begotten cannot be coeval with the one by whom it is begotten. Therefore, neither is the Son coeternal with the Father," there Augustine rightly sets against them the fact that the emanation of the sun's rays is coeval with the sun, etc.

CHAPTER 2.

THE ABUSE OF PHILOSOPHY IN THEOLOGY.

There are many uses of philosophy in theology, but there are many destructive abuses of it as well which we will reduce to the same headings in order to show how, in the organic, confirming, and refuting use, philosophy is turned into abuse.

In the *organic use,* the following abuses occur: (1) When that preparation of the mind that will be cultivated through the study of philosophy is stated to be the beginning of saving faith and is judged to coincide effectively with the inner illumination of the Holy Spirit. Keckermann (libr. 1. *System. Theol.* cap. 4. p. 57.): "Through those two plainly different disciplines of metaphysics and logic, God wants to kindle the light of the Holy Spirit in the minds of men." But that divine inner effect and spiritual illumination of the mind is nowhere in Scripture attributed to the medium of philosophy, but only to the revealed Word (Psa. 19:9, Psa. 119:105, 2 Pet. 1:19, etc.), for which reason Savonarola correctly writes (*de scient. divis.* lib. 3. p. 809): "If anyone were to diligently consider the Holy Scripture with purity of heart, good works, contemplation, and the illumination of the Holy Spirit rather than with the power of natural ability and the exercise of human study, he will learn. Surely if these sciences were so necessary that the Christian Republic could not thrive without them, our Lord

Christ would not have left out these disciplines from His or His Apostles' teaching." Keckermann (lib. 1. *praecogn. Philos.* cap. 4. p. 80.): "Piety—the worship and honor and invocation of God—is said to be awakened in us through philosophy." But true piety, the worship of God, and the invocation that is pleasing to God cannot take place apart from knowledge of Christ the Mediator, which philosophy cannot attain. John 5:23: "He who does not honor the Son also does not honor the Father." John 14:6: "No one comes to the Father except through Me." To this pertains the error of Cinglius, Gualterus, Bullingerus, Andradius, Thamerus, Erasmus, Galeotus Martius, Puccius, and others who grant eternal salvation to the Gentiles who search for God from the book of Nature and who live according to the precept of right reason, which opposes the records of divine truth in many ways. Pareus (in *Iren.* cap. 24. pag. 245.) laments that this "slander" is attributed to Cinglius, since "he wrote it under a certain condition," namely, "on the chance that they might depart from here in faith." But where could faith come from in the minds of the Gentiles apart from the knowledge of the Gospel and Christ? Psalm 36:10: "In Your light we see light." 1 Cor. 1:21: "The world through wisdom did not know God." Rom. 10:17: "Faith comes from hearing (that is, the hearing of the Word)," not from philosophical reasoning. The Jesuit Roestius (in *Pseudojub.* cap. 9. p. 74.) writes: "Christ and the Apostles defeated their enemies by using the things included in technical Dialectic and especially in the so-called Aristotelian instrument." But from whence will the Sophist prove that Christ and the Apostles used that technical Dialectic?

(2) When in the explanation of terms a certain mastery is assigned to philosophy and it is required that the theologian insecurely entrust to philosophy the judgment concerning

the terms taken up from philosophy, even though those terms that have been received into the holy city of God are rather often clothed with a new meaning whenever one must learn to speak in new languages in the Church. Thus it is an abuse of philosophy when the Papists want to prove from the grammatical composition of a word that justification consists in the infusion of righteousness and in the production of righteous works. We have adduced many examples of this abuse above.

(3) When logic no longer serves and acts as a handmaid, but dominates theology, that is, when it forms arguments against theological assertions from its own topical rules and, contrary to the proper manner of education, switches to a different genre. This is sacred to the Scholastics, who are used to arguing from the principles of logic, importing their conclusions from there. Therefore, after posing their questions, they submit logical axioms and topical maxims, or even something less than that, as Sadeel writes about them (in *praefation. de method disputandi*). Petrus Damianus argues thus against this abuse (*ad Desiderium Abb. Cassienensem lib. de omnipotent. Dei c. 5.*): "Clearly these things which proceed from the arguments of Dialectics or Rhetoricians should not be readily applied to the divine mysteries, nor should they turn the things invented for this purpose only into instruments of the Syllogists or into the conclusions of speeches, without resolutely going back to the Holy Scriptures and contrasting the necessities of their conclusion with the divine truth. Nevertheless, this skill of human art, if used for sacred speech, should not usurp for itself the boast of mastery, but as a handmaid it should aid its mistress with a certain familial service, lest in taking the lead it should lead astray, and while following the consequences of the external words, it should lose the light of inner truth and the straight path of the truth."

In the *confirming use*, these abuses occur: (1) When a person depends on philosophical reasoning to confirm the lofty mysteries of the faith, while leaving out the singular principle of theology, which is the Word of God. Scotus, Raymond de Sabaude, and others attempt in this way to deduce the mystery of the Trinity from the principles of philosophy.

(2) When the testimonies of Scripture are placed after philosophical reasoning, as if the proof were more certain through philosophical arguments than through the sayings of Scripture. Thus Keckermann, as he is about to demonstrate the Trinity of Persons from the properties of intelligent Nature, begins in this way: "We shall openly prove to the Antitrinitarians that the Trinity of Persons flows forth from the very essence of God, and that God cannot be God unless He has three distinct modes of existence or Persons. In demonstrating this, we shall also produce testimonies from the Holy Scriptures." With these words, he clearly places his philosophical discourse before the divine testimonies. Thus the Scholastics often begin by disputing the articles of faith at length from philosophical reasoning and from the sayings of Aristotle, and only afterwards, for the sake of appearance, bring in the passages of Scripture.

(3) When saving faith is judged to be established and confirmed by philosophical reasoning, although there can be no firmer proof of faith than the authority of God, who speaks in the Scriptures and through the Scriptures, for God is truth itself, and His Word is of the most certain and steadfast truth. Indeed, it is firmer than heaven and earth.

(4) When in 'mixed questions' (as they are called), that is, questions in which one term is philosophical and the other

theological, it is stated that the confirming arguments can be sought from philosophy. Alstedius (in *praecogn. Theol.* p. 684.): "When the questions are mixed, let the reasons sought from the light of Nature be admitted." Keckermann states the same thing (libr. 3. *syst. Log.* tract. 1. sect. 2. cap. 9.), against which Dr. Meisner rightly argues thus (in *quaestione de usu Philosophiae part. 1. sobriae Phil.* p. 27.): "When, in conclusions, terms are not employed that are simple in and of themselves, but rather are connected in such a way that a judgment can only be rendered in these mixed questions by that discipline which does not deal separately with each term, but rather with the connection of the terms and their mutual association, only theology is of such a kind, not philosophy. Therefore, judgment must be pronounced in questions of this kind from theology alone, not from philosophy." Briefly, the answer to a question requires a knowledge both of the subject and of the predicate, and, of course, of the connection that comes between them. But in mixed questions, philosophy does not have both terms, namely, the subject and the predicate, nor has it learned the connection between the subject and the predicate. Therefore.

Here is a mixed question: Is the body of Christ in only one place? The answer to this question cannot be sought from philosophy, because philosophy, although it deals with location, does not deal at all with the body of Christ. It deals with the natural body, but the body of Christ is not merely and purely natural, but glorified. Indeed, it is the very body of the Logos, in view of which its condition is unknown to all human reason and thus also to philosophy. Nor is there any merit to the distinction between *philosophy considered only in itself vs. philosophy enlightened by the light of grace*, because philosophy enlightened by the light of grace no longer renders judgment in theological questions from its own principles, but from the Word of God, knowing that it must be done in this way. Nor does philosophy employ theology as a science subordinate to itself. On the contrary, philosophy is subordinate to theology and is employed by theology in its own service. The light of Nature does not produce the light of grace, but the light of grace produces the light of Nature.

In the *refuting use* of philosophy, many abuses occur. (1) When philosophical axioms are accepted as general axioms and are set against the mysteries of the faith, even though they are specific axioms and only hold true in their own sphere. Thus physics teaches that *a natural body cannot be in many places at the same time*, which is true in the sphere of physics, that is, when the question deals with a natural body and the power of Nature. But when the Calvinists attempt to infer from this principle that *the body of Christ cannot be present in the Holy Supper,* they are accepting a philosophical axiom as absolutely universal, and they are wickedly setting it against the mystery of faith.

(2) When the judgment concerning a real contradiction in the mysteries of faith is entrusted to human reason. It is certainly true that, in an absolute and simple sense, God does not make any contradictions.* And thus it is also true that, in

---

* The Scholastics prove this with the following reasoning. Since God is the highest and most perfect Entity, and when He makes all things, He makes them like Himself, the action of God Himself cannot, in itself, extend to any non-Entity. But in every contradiction there is a non-Entity, because in every contradiction there is something true and something false. But that which is false is a non-Entity. And a non-Entity is incompatible with God, nor does it have similarity with Him. (Thomas 1. q. 25. art. 3.) If God could do the things that imply contradiction, He could make a false sentence true. But falsehood is contrary to God, for He is truth itself.

an absolute and simple sense, a so-called contradiction cannot exist in the divine mysteries. But one neither can nor should use rational principles to determine what things are truly contradictory in the articles of faith; one should only come to a conclusion in this matter based on the revealed Word. But since this practice is not observed by our Calvinist and Photinian adversaries, that is why those things are considered contradictory which, in fact, are not contradictory in an absolute and simple sense. Thus it seems to the Calvinists to be contradictory that the body of Christ is a real body and that it is present in many places; that the human nature of Christ is truly human and that it has personally been made a participant in the divine attributes. Therefore, they attack the latter based on the former. "The things that imply contradiction are not contained under divine power."* To the Photinians it seems contradictory that God is one and that in the divine Essence there are three Persons; that Christ is true Man and true God in the unity of the Person. Therefore, they also attack the latter based on the former. But we respond most simply that those things are truly contradictory which are contradictory, not by the judgment of human reason, but by the judgment of the Holy Spirit speaking in the Scriptures. But these things just mentioned above are contradictory, not by the judgment of the Holy Spirit, but only by the judgment of reason, for the Holy Spirit teaches both things in the Scriptures; namely, that the body of Christ

---

* Goclenus (in *disq. Phil.* 4:29.): "It is not proper to argue from the omnipotence of God in order to confirm that which implies contradiction." Sadeel (*de sacr. mand.* p. 86.): "If something is advanced that is contrary to Nature and overturns it, it is immediately judged to be false." (pag. 273. Mich. Philipp. Beuterus *de vera dijud. contro. relig. theorem.* 24. & 25.): "He proposes that analogy of faith as a standard in theological disputes between which and human reason no contradiction is implied."

is a real body and that the body of Christ is present in many places, etc. Therefore, these things are not truly, absolutely, and simply contradictory.

Furthermore, that judgment concerning a true contradiction in the articles of faith is not to be entrusted to human reason can be demonstrated with many foundational truths. (1) The divine mysteries have been placed beyond the grasp of reason. Therefore, reason neither can nor should judge concerning either the truth or falsehood of those things, and consequently it cannot make a judgment about a contradiction in them. Scaliger (exerc. 77. sect. 2.): "I conclude that those things which are beyond Nature should also not be judged by the laws of Nature." In the same place: "Divine power is not to be measured by the ten-foot-pole of our reason." (exer. 365.): "Man would never have enough blessed natural capacity to learn all the magnificent, enormous, immense things about the ineffable omnipotence of God." Here observe that, when we say that the mysteries of faith have been placed beyond the grasp of reason, it should not be taken merely in the sense that reason, apart from revelation of the Word, cannot attain the knowledge of them, but also that, even with the revelation of the Word, reason is still unable to understand them completely, and thus it is also unable to conclude from its own principles what parts of the mysteries of faith are to be considered truly contradictory. To this pertain all the passages of Scripture in which the articles of faith are called 'mysteries,' for they are so called because they exceed all grasp of human reason, which is the peculiar nature of mysteries (Eph. 3:8–9; 1 Cor. 2:7, 14–16; 1 Tim. 6:16). Justin (in ἔκθ. πιστ. p. 307.): "They are beyond our mind, beyond our speech, beyond our grasp." Bernard (*Epist. 190 ad Innocentium de Abailardo*): "As he is prepared to give a reason for everything, even those things which are beyond reason, he presumes both against reason and against faith. For what is more contrary to reason than to attempt to transcend reason with reason? And what is more contrary to faith than to be unwilling to believe that which you cannot grasp with reason?"

There is someone among the Christian Philosophers who observes this distinction. "There are two kinds of mysteries. One has to do with those things of which it can be known from Nature, not that they exist, but that they can exist, such as the resurrection of the dead, the creation of something from nothing, and similar things. For it is certainly possible for us not to view the latter things as contradictions, since we understand the former terms. The other kind of mystery has to do with the things of which it can neither be known that they exist nor that they can exist, that is, of the things of which reason is altogether ignorant with regard to whether or not they imply a contradiction. To this pertains the mystery of the Trinity, for reason cannot even imagine what those three Persons are. How can it know, then, whether they exist or not?" However much these mysteries, with respect to the first kind, seem to involve something doubtful, however much it may be true with the example of the Photinians that those kinds of mysteries involve a contradiction according to the judgment of reason, nevertheless, with respect to the second kind, they are altogether immovable matters of truth.

(2) Reason and Mistress Philosophy cannot make a judgment about the power of God as to what it can or cannot accomplish. Therefore, it also cannot judge what things are truly contradictory in the divine mysteries. The antecedent is clear from many Scripture passages. (Gen. 18:14; Zec. 8:6; Mat. 19:26; Luke 1:38; Luke 18:26.) Especially to be noted is

the declaration of the Apostle in Ephesians 3:20: "God is powerful to do above all things superabundantly more than we ask or understand." If God can do those things which surpass our understanding, then certainly He is also able to do those things which imply a contradiction in our logic. If God can do all things with His absolute power, certainly nothing possible is excepted, or else it would show that God is not able to do it by His absolute power. If God is able to do things that are impossible with men, He can also do things that are impossible with our reason, for what else does 'with men' mean but with our reason? For we are discussing not only things that are impossible to do, but also to imagine. One must distinguish, therefore, between the *ordinary* and the *absolute* power of God, for the latter can do those things which seem to us to involve a contradiction, for God is not bound, in His absolute power, to the logical contradiction and to the law of human reason. One must distinguish between a contradiction of divine logic, that is, the logic of God, which far transcends our grasp, and a contradiction of human logic, that is, of man, which does not transcend human grasp. One must distinguish between the things or utterances which are beyond the boundaries of logic, that is, of our reason, and those which are within the boundaries of our logic and can be perceived by our reason. Augustine (lib. 21. *de civ. Dei* cap. 5. near the end): "The lowest reason of mortals is vanquished by the wondrous works of God, and yet reason is firmly established in us, that the Almighty works not without reason, from whence the infirm human mind is unable to grasp the reason; and that, indeed, we are uncertain of what He wills in many things, and yet this is most certain: that none of the things that He has willed is impossible for Him, and that we believe Him when He speaks; we are able to believe Him to be neither powerless nor a liar." (cap. 7.): "Since

God is the Author of nature, why do they want us to give a stronger reason, when they do not want to believe anything to be impossible? And to those who demand an explanation of the reason, we respond that this is the will of the Almighty God, who certainly is not called Almighty for any other reason than that He is able to do whatever He wills." Thomas (liber. 1. *contra gentes* cap. 3.) proceeds in this way: "The intellect, which is not infinite, is in no way capable of penetrating that which is infinite. No creature's human intellect is infinite, but falls upon God alone. Therefore, no creature in general fully understands God, which is why so many things about God's nature must still lie altogether hidden from us." (God's power is infinite, having no limit, transcending the grasp of reason. Therefore, although reason may wish to limit it for us and may wish to say that God can do all possible things, Scripture speaks differently: "Nothing is impossible with God, etc.") In addition, the infinite God knows and can accomplish much more than the angels, and the angels much more than man. Therefore, human intellect is not and cannot be the rule of divine power. But if anyone resists or denies the things which are placed in Holy Scripture to be believed because they go beyond our grasp and seem impossible and even contradictory, he takes up for himself the judgment about God's power and presumptuously concludes that God cannot do more than human reason understands to be possible.

Alstedius retorts (libr. 2. *praecogn. Theol.* c. 10. p. 72.): "Everything that implies contradiction with respect to right reason also implies contradiction with respect to God. For what is right, true, and good in the creatures is a certain trace of Him who is the highest right, true, and good. Therefore, if right reason rightly judges that something implies a contradiction, this rightness will be in accord with the highest rightness, which is God Himself, not contrary to it."

We reply: Reason is only right and only judges rightly in divine matters when it judges, not from its own principles, but from the Word, which things are impossible with God and contradictory. That the rectitude* in the creatures is a trace of the rectitude in God is not absolutely, simply, and entirely true, but according to what is also said in particular, that is, the rectitude in the creatures is a trace, not of every power, but of the ordinary power of God. Meanwhile, concerning the extent of the absolute power of God, no judgment can be made from that trace of rectitude in the creatures, that is, from the effects of His ordinary power. Ordinary power does not exhaust the whole power of God, but is like a portion of it. Many things are done by God beyond the laws of created Nature. Where God wills, the order of Nature is overturned.

Alstedius again retorts (in the same place, p.74): "The principles of Nature are a ray of the wisdom and truth of God. There is, then, no clash between them and the divine concepts. Indeed, the truth of those principles is conformity with the primary One and True."

We reply: There is no clash between the principles of Nature and the revealed Word in and of themselves, as long as the principles of Nature are subject to the revealed Word. But if someone wants to argue against the revealed Word from the principles of Nature, he uses the ordinary power of God to attack His absolute power. He wants to judge the immense light from the rays, the whole fountain from the little drops. The principles of Nature certainly conform to the first Truth, and

---

*   *rectum*

yet, at the same time, they do not comprehend or exhaust His infinite wisdom and power.

(3) Human reason is blinded through and after the Fall, obscured with vanity, errors, and darkness in judging divine and spiritual matters. Therefore, it is dangerous to allow it to judge contradiction in the mysteries of faith. The antecedent is clear from Rom. 1:21; 1 Cor. 1:19; Eph. 4:17, etc. If even that which has to do with natural things is poorly discerned, like a night raven in the dark, how much less can human reason provide an infallible judgment when it comes to divine matters? Wisdom 9:16: "With difficulty do we esteem the things on the earth, and the things in plain sight we discover with toil. But the things that are in heaven, who will investigate?" John 3:12: "If I tell you earthly things and you do not believe, how will you believe if I tell you heavenly things?" Compare Aristotle (lib. 2. *Methaph.* cap. 1.), Scaliger (exerc. 1. sect. 1.). Luis Vives beautifully expresses (in comm. lib. 20. *de civ. Dei* cap. 20.) the words of Augustine: "The resurrection of the dead is to be believed, although we do not comprehend it, since it is in the future." Vives adds: "This is one of the dogmas of piety, this 'it is to be believed,' this 'it is to be maintained.' The reason, as being in the future, we leave to God and we bow our necks under the easy yoke of Christ, in obedience to God. It is enough for the Christian to believe that this or that is, will be, or was. Let him leave it to God to know the causes and reasons for all things, for He was not willing that even the clearest and brightest matters of Nature should be clear and bright to us."

(4) We are commanded to take reason captive under the obedience of Christ (2 Cor. 10:5). Therefore, we should not grant it the judicial privileges concerning contradiction in articles of faith. The connection is obvious. For if reason could

or should judge truth and falsehood, and likewise could judge contradiction in the things that are declared to be mysteries, then to what end was it commanded to be taken captive under the obedience of Christ?

(5) If judgment over matters of faith and over contradiction in those matters is granted to reason and to philosophy, the Prince of Reason, it will pronounce sentence against many mysteries of faith revealed in Scripture.

From those principles: "Those who differ in person do not have the same essence in number. Whatever is the foundation of a relation is an accident. No relation that distinguishes is, for that very reason, the same as the essence which it distinguishes. If a person adds nothing real to the essence, the persons are not really distinguished. But if it adds something more, a combination must exist. If the Son was begotten by the Father, He must also depend on Him, and thus He cannot be God. The breathing* in the Father is either the same as the generation or it is something else. If the Son does not breathe first, since He does not generate; if He breathes second, there must be a peculiar personal property, and thus there must be four persons." From these, I say, and from similar philosophical declarations, reason will judge that the Trinity of Persons in the Divinity must be denied.

From those principles: "Disparity cannot be affirmatively predicted of disparity by a proper enunciation. The finite is not capable of the infinite. No subsistence** really differs from that Nature of which it is a subsistence. The finite does not subsist except by a finite person, etc." Reason will judge that the

---

*	*spiratio*
**	*hypostasis*

mystery of the incarnation must be denied. If you should say that *reason or philosophy enlightened by the revelation of the Word and by the efficacy of the Holy Spirit can explain all things in such a way that no contradiction seems to remain,* I reply in brief with those who have learned the mystery of the Trinity from Scripture and who believe it with steadfast faith: that those answers and limitations certainly exist, but the adversaries, who attack this mystery from their principles, always find something to retort, nor do they allow themselves to be satisfied with those explanations and limitations, as is apparent from Keckermann's dissertation on this mystery from the principles of philosophy, and from the refutation of the Photinian Adam Goslavus de Bebelno which was opposed to him. The safest thing, then, is to send the philosophical pronouncements made by the adversaries against the mysteries of faith back to their own sphere and to ponder and discuss those lofty mysteries of the faith from the Holy Scriptures alone, which are the only proper principle of theology and which alone provide an immovable and unalterable foundation. Epiphanius (*haeres.* 65.): "We take on the discovery of each and every question, not from our own reason, but from the logical consequence of the Scriptures." Chrystostom (*homil. 5. in 1. Timot.*): "Human reason has nothing in common with the divine. Therefore, it is blasphemy to wish to discuss divine matters with reason." From the same author (*homil. 5. in Corinth.*): "To want to understand divine matters from philosophy is like wanting to handle glowing-hot iron, not with tongs, but with one's fingers."

Furthermore, a philosopher does not offer those limitations and explanations of philosophical axioms as a philosopher, from the principles of his own knowledge, because his own knowledge ignores the divine mysteries. How, then, will he limit his axioms on their account? But he does it as a Christian, or rather, as a theologian, using the principles of theology, and thus they are no longer axioms of philosophy, but, in a certain respect, of theology.

But why would we want to introduce that confusion of philosophy and theology[*], which long ago existed in the Church as a fount of all evil? Why would we want to reinstate the Scholastic Theology in our churches which Blessed Luther expelled from them with such great toil and sweat, as if to grant it the right to return home, placing it again on the theological throne with applause? Is it not preferable and far more prudent to leave it to philosophy to explain, limit, and form its own axioms from the light of Nature, and not to discuss the divine mysteries placed beyond all reason and philosophy, except from the revealed Word? We are opposed to Alstedius, then, when he (libr. 2. cap. 109. p. 247.) forms these theses which he says are to be observed, if the sayings of Scripture seem to clash with reason. "(1) One should not judge the essence of God from human reason or from the order of Nature. Why? Because the Author of Nature is not subject to those laws which He prescribed for Nature, but transcends it in infinite ways. (2) God is the freest Agent. Therefore, He does not always act in one and the same manner. (3) God is all-wise. Therefore, whatever He does, it is not fitting to argue for any imperfection, as such as it may appear so to corrupt reason. (4) God is omnipotent, and thus all Nature is under His power, so that He is able to govern and alter it as He sees fit." He is quite right about these things, but they are not at all consistent with the things which we set forth from him above. This is our opinion: If those philosophical axioms which are

---

[*]   μιξοφιλοσοφοθεολογίαν or *mixophilosophotheology*

asserted by the adversaries for attacking the heavenly truth can be limited and explained from the very principles of philosophy, we do not disapprove those limitations and explanations. For example, when they attack the real communication of the divine attributes to the flesh of Christ on the basis of the philosophical axiom, *one's own character cannot be communicated**, the axiom is rightly limited from the very principles of philosophy by distinguishing between communication according to participation and according to combination,** and likewise by demonstrating the contrary with examples of red-hot iron and an animate body.

But when such axioms which cannot be limited and explained from the principles of philosophy are asserted, it is preferable to relegate those things to the philosophical sphere and simply to repudiate them in a discussion of the lofty mysteries of faith than to explain them with painstaking limitations, in order that there be an abridgment of the disputation and that the adversaries and guests may be forcibly drawn to the proper principle for discussing these mysteries, namely, the Holy Scriptures. For example, when a Photinian argues in this way: "A personal property in the Father is either the same as the essence, or in reality distinct from it. If the former, then the persons of the Trinity are not really different; if the latter, then there must a combination in God." In this case it is preferable to call the adversary back to the sayings of Scripture which fully and plainly instruct us in this mystery, than to painstakingly question whether a personal property is really, or formally, or rationally distinguished from the essence of the Father. For if you said anything of the sort, the persistent adversary would

---

*   *proprium non potest communicari*
**   κατὰ μέθεξιν καὶ κατὰ συνδύασιν

find something to throw back at you from reason. Therefore, it is safest and simplest to answer that the philosophical axioms are not to be applied, outside of its sphere and against educational propriety, to the lofty mysteries revealed in Scripture which are incomprehensible to human reason, namely, in such a way as to be attacked from them.

Of all these things that have been said about the use and abuse of philosophy in theology, the most important is that philosophy is not to be granted the mastery in theology, but the ministry, as Philo declares (in *lib. de Cherubin.*) with this comparison: "Theology is like Sarah in the house of her lord. Philosophy is admitted as a slave and a handmaid, who takes on the role of Hagar in the house of Abraham." Luther used to compare philosophy to a donkey, and the theologian to Christ riding on the donkey. He says: "The donkey is not placed on Christ, but Christ on the donkey." Aristotle himself grants (2. *Metaph.*) that his Ethical Philosophy is "the most sovereign and authoritative; the other sciences, as slaves, may not rightly contradict it."

CHAPTER 3.

THE TOOLS OF THE STUDY OF PHILOSOPHY.

We presuppose, at this point, the knowledge of philosophy in the one to whom we wish to pass on the method of theological study. Therefore, it would be foolish to treat broadly the tools for learning philosophy. For the moment, we briefly suggest the following.

(1) Aristotelian Philosophy is preferable to the rest, both on account of the more perfect reason for philosophizing and on account of the adversaries, with whom the theologian must descend into the arena, for most of them use (and also abuse) Aristotelian Philosophy. Meanwhile, we do not disapprove, if Aristotelian and Ramaean Philosophies are combined for the sake of comparison and method.

(2) The one who desires a more accurate knowledge of philosophy should approach the reading of Aristotle himself. It is better to drink from the fountain than to pursue the little brooks that are often murky and muddy.

(3) One should read from the translations of Zabarella for clarity, of Scaliger for subtlety.

(4) As in all things, so especially in the study of philosophy, all things should be reduced to their beneficial use,

avoiding thorny, futile, and useless questions. The course of life is brief; it hardly grants sufficient time for learning the things that are necessary.

(5) In any branch of philosophy, but especially in metaphysics and logic, the explanations of terms, the useful distinctions, and the canons or axioms should be observed, which, rendered under certain titles, provide great benefit in disputations. Dr. Sagittarius provides an excellent service in this regard.

(6) The practice of debating, offered in due time, is very helpful for an accurate knowledge of philosophy.

(7) In every branch of philosophy, a certain author should be chosen with whom a person familiarizes himself by daily reading. It is readily understood that this author must be ahead of the rest in being clear, vigorous, accurate, and foundational. But to whom this praise applies in every branch of philosophy will be taught by those to whom this supervision properly belongs. Here we ourselves will signal the retreat and cross over to our camp.

Part Three.

Fruitfully Completing the Course of Theological Study.

We have finally entered the inner sanctuary of theology through the exterior courtyard of languages and philosophy. It remains for us, then, diligently to contemplate everything in it that pertains to the sacred furnishings of theological education. He who has been instructed with the necessary knowledge of the languages and the arts, having presented and daily repeated his serious prayers to God, being faithfully informed and led by the hand, having also shown due diligence over the space of five years, the Lord blessings his labors, is able to acquire such success in theology that the entrance to the highest degree in it lies open to him. This is why such a long span of time spent on this queen of all disciplines is required of the candidates in the statutes of the Theological Faculty.

Nevertheless, no one should be disturbed when he hears 'the space of five years' or when he thinks about explaining the length of this study in the following years, for, as the definitions, so also the canons and rules are passed on with regard to the ideal. If he is not given to be carried forward to that ideal of perfection, it is sufficient if he makes some progress; if he is not permitted to aspire to the first tiers, it is laudable to subsist in the second or even the third. In the Levitical tabernacle there were not only chief priests, but also inferior Levites—indeed, even doorkeepers. Yet all were admitted to the holy things. So it is in the study of theology that not all who are devoted to it are able to make equal progress, for which reason even the ecclesiastical offices are not equal. Nevertheless, there will be no one who, equipped with average talent, is unable, through prayers and toil, to furnish something worthy of love and praise, if he observes the due order of studies and puts some time into the academic exercises.

Section 1: The first year of theological study.

Chapter 1.

The necessity and utility of diligently and regularly reading the Holy Scripture.

After the serious invocation of God, no tool of theological study is more necessary and useful than the diligent and regular reading of Holy Scripture. (1) The salutary knowledge of God is not born in our minds or with our minds, but is only sought and drawn from the revealed Word (Mat. 11:26, 16:17; John 1:18; 2 Tim. 3:15; 2 Pet. 1:19, etc.) (2) God, having been invoked by pious prayers, wants to kindle the salutary knowledge of Himself by the efficacy of the Holy Spirit, yet not immediately, but through hearing, reading, and meditating on the Word (Psa. 119:105; Pro. 6:23; Luke 24:32; Acts 16:14). (3) Just as we speak with God through prayer, so through His Word, God speaks with us. Prayers are the channels through which heavenly wisdom is drawn to us; the Word is the fountain of that wisdom from which it is drawn. The Word is the light of the mind, the medicine of the soul, the mirror in which the face of God appears. It is the bread that nourishes the soul.

It is the sword with which we can fight against the adversaries. It is the Lydian stone according to which all dogmas are to be examined. (4) Holy Scripture is the only proper principle of theology from which alone firm and convincing arguments in theological questions are made. But when it comes to learning well the principles of any science, great study is normally employed. (5) Holy Scripture is perfect (Psa. 19:7). It announces the whole plan of God concerning our salvation (Acts 20:27; 26:22). It can make us wise for salvation (2 Tim. 3:15). Who can doubt, then, that the regular and daily reading of Scripture is highly necessary for the future theologian? (The compelling reasons for frequently and regularly reading the Bible are common and particular. The common reasons concern all Christians, such as the divine authority of this book [2 Tim. 3:16], the severity of the divine command [Deu. 6:6, Col. 3:16], the grandeur of the mysteries set forth in this book [1 Cor. 2:6], the utility of reading, etc. The particular reason, with the theologian in view, is set forth in 2 Tim. 3:16.) (6) For this reason, in addition to prayer, the royal Prophet, by his example, commends to us the reading of Scripture and meditation on it. Psalm 119:13: "I have declared with my lips all the judgments of Your mouth." V. 16: "I will meditate on Your statutes; I will not forget Your words." V. 48: "I have lifted up my hands to Your commandments, which I have loved; and I will train in Your statutes." V. 97: "Oh, how I love Your Law; it is my meditation all the day." V. 148: "My eyes precede the watches in order to meditate on Your Word." Psalm 1:2 pronounces him blessed who "meditates on the Law of the Lord day and night." Christ, in John 5:39, commands all those who are truly pious, but especially those who have been admitted to the sacred things, to "search the Scriptures." Timothy, Bishop of the Church at Ephesus, knew the Holy Scriptures from the time he was a boy (2 Tim. 3:1), and yet he is commanded by the Apostle to attend to reading (1 Tim. 4:13). (Alfonso, King of Spain and Naples, boasted that he had read through the Bible fourteen times, together with the usual glosses and the commentaries of Lyra and the additions of Paul of Burgos.)

CHAPTER 2.

HOW THE HOLY SCRIPTURE IS TO BE READ.

Many read the Scripture, but without fruit. Some also read it as the expense of their own salvation and the salvation of others; namely, those who seek in it and extract from it support for their own preconceived errors, as a spider extracts its venom from a rose. Therefore, the Scripture must be read:

(1) First, with serious prayers sent to God that He would open our eyes to consider the mysteries of the divine Word. (2) With a spirit of learning and drawing from the Scriptures the sense of its sayings, not with a spirit of bringing one's own preconceived notions into them. Hilary (lib. 1. *de Trinit*. fol. 7.):"The best reader of Scripture is he who draws out the understanding of its sayings from its sayings, not he who imports his own understanding into it; he who brings from it, not he who brings to it, nor he who compels its passages to contain only that which he, before reading, had presumed to understand." (3) With a humble and submissive mind, that we may reflect upon the fact that the divine Majesty, before whom the angels hide their faces, is speaking to us. To read the sacred things is to stand before God and to hear Him teaching about eternal salvation. (4) With the steady purpose of taking captive one's understanding under the obedience of Christ and of believing the words of God, although they may seem absurd and

incongruous to our reason. Chrysostom (homil. 21. in *Genesis*): "When God pronounces something, His words should not be contradicted. Even if the things that God pronounces do not harmonize with what the eyes observe, God's pronouncements are to be considered all the more trustworthy." (5) With a fervent spirit, not lazily or with a wandering mind (Rom. 12:11). The incense of prayer will kindle this fervor of spirit. (6) Frequently and regularly. For it is not sufficient to read the Scripture now and again; the reading of Scripture must be repeated, continued, and daily fomented. Augustine (Epist. 3. *ad Volusianum*, not far from the beginning): "So great is the profundity of the Christian writings that in them I would daily advance, if only I might endeavor, from the beginning of youth until decrepit old age, with utmost tranquility, with the highest zeal, with better talent, to learn them alone; not that it is so difficult to arrive at the things in them that are necessary for salvation, but because there each one has grasped the faith without which one cannot live piously and uprightly. So many things remain, with so many shady retreats of mysteries casting shadows over the understanding. So much depth of wisdom lies hidden, not only in the words with which those things have been said, but also in the matters which are to be understood, so that, to the most aged, to the most acute, to those most ardent in passion for learning, it happens as the Scripture itself says in a certain place: When a man has finished, then he has just begun." The Rabbis say correctly: "There is not an *iota* in the Scripture on which mountains of doctrine do not depend." The Holy Scripture is a sea whose profundity cannot be explored by us in this life, much less exhausted, for which reason, in Eze. 47:5, a Prophet is prefigured in a river, crossing one part of it up to his ankles, but the other part he could not enter because of its depth. Gregory (homil. 7. in *Ezech.*): "The divine discussions with the reader grow, for the more deeply each one strains in them, the more deeply he understands them." The Scripture is the rock which is not accustomed to pour out the water of doctrine unless we strike it by frequently reading, meditating, and praying. Therefore, Blessed Luther is right when he makes the grave assessment of the 'praiseworthy' wisdom of those who, after one reading of some Biblical pericope, immediately promised that they had a perfect knowledge of it. He says: "Beware, lest some tedium and contempt creeps up on you in reading the Holy Scriptures, or else you will never be able to reach the goal of theological study. You will never be too diligent in reading the Scriptures, and the things which you diligently read you will never understand too accurately. The things which you understand rightly, you will never teach others too faithfully. The things which you teach most faithfully, you will never express too zealously with the example of your life."

So that the student of theology may be able to move about the more fruitfully and easily in the reading of Scripture, he should divide his reading into cursory and accurate manners of reading. We will deal with each kind individually.

CHAPTER 3.

THE CURSORY READING OF SCRIPTURE.

With the title, 'cursory reading,' we certainly do not mean to imply that the Bible should only be read hastily, without study and attention, as a fleeing dog drinks from the Nile, but we call it a cursory reading with respect to the so-called accurate reading. In such a cursory reading, we run through the chapters of the Bible several times daily in the vernacular or Latin language, without inspecting or comparing the original languages, without noting the emphases and without using the commentaries of the interpreters, so that the text of the Scripture may become familiar to us, for that is easily the primary aim of such reading. The following rules should be observed in this cursory reading:

(1) The division of cursory reading. Cursory reading should be separated into a *morning* and an *evening* reading.

For the morning reading, these books should be assigned: Genesis (50 chapters); Job (42 chapters); the Psalter (150 Psalms); Proverbs (31 chapters); Ecclesiastes (12 chapters); Song of Solomon (8 chapters); the four major Prophets: Isaiah (66 chapters), Jeremiah (52 chapters), Lamentations (5 chapters), Ezekiel (48 chapters), Daniel (12 chapters); the twelve minor Prophets: Hosea (14 chapters), Joel (3 chapters),

Amos (9 chapters), Obadiah (1 chapters), Jonah (4 chapters), Micah (7 chapters), Nahum (3 chapters), Habakkuk (3 chapters), Zephaniah (3 chapters), Haggai (2 chapters), Zechariah (14 chapters), Malachi (4 chapters); the Apostolic Epistles in the New Testament. These books contain, in total, 665 chapters.

For the evening reading, the following are assigned: Exodus (40 chapters); Leviticus (27 chapters); Numbers (36 chapters); Deuteronomy (34 chapters); Joshua (24 chapters); Judges (21 chapters); Ruth (4 chapters); 1 Samuel (31 chapters); 2 Samuel (24 chapters); 1 Kings (22 chapters); 2 Kings (25 chapters); 1 Chronicles (29 chapters); 2 Chronicles (36 chapters); Ezra (10 chapters); Nehemiah (13 chapters); Esther (10 chapters); and likewise the Apocryphal books: Judith (16 chapters), Wisdom (19 chapters), Tobit (14 chapters), Sirach (51 chapters), Baruch (6 chapters), 1 Maccabees (16 chapters), 2 Maccabees (15 chapters), the fragments of Esther (9 chapters), Daniel's Bel and the Dragon (5 chapters), the Prayer of Azariah, the Song of the Three Youths, the Prayer of Manasseh (1 chapter), 1 Esdras (9 chapters), 2 Esdras (16 chapters); from the New Testament, the four Evangelists, the Acts of the Apostles, the Revelation of John. These books similarly contain 670 chapters.

We assign one set of books for the morning and the other for the evening reading because the books of the first class are mostly didactic and thus require more attention, which is stronger in us in the morning. But the books of the second class are mostly historical and thus do not require as much straining of the mind as the first, except for Revelation. (If the Psalms that are read are not counted separately, then there are 777 chapters of the Canonical Old Testament books. If a person were to read through fifteen chapters per week, that is, two chapters every day and three on the seventh day, then all the books of the Old Testament will be finished precisely once in the span of a year, with three days left over. If you wanted to multiply the number of chapters so that you could run through those books of the Old Testament as often as two or three times a year, it would be easy to reckon. There are, in all, 260 chapters of the New Testament. If five chapters of the New Testament are read each week, it will be finished in precisely twelve months. If ten chapters are read per week, it will be completed twice in the course of the year.)

(2) All counted, there are 1,335 chapters of all the books of the Old and New Testaments. If a person finishes reading two chapters of Scripture in the morning and two in the evening, he will have read through the whole Bible in 333-1/2 days, and thus there will still be 32 days left over, in case, on account of unexpected affairs that arise, the allotted time for reading could not be completed from time to time. But if a person is even more diligent and reads through two chapters in the morning, two before lunch, and two in the evening, he will arrive at the goal in 222 days.

(3) *Order.* Since the New Testament is the explanation of the Old, one should begin his cursory reading from the books of the New Testament. The Old Testament Apocrypha are placed at the end, or the Canonical books can even be read twice before the Apocryphal books are read once.

(4) Some prescribe the reading of the Biblical books according to the historical order, for which reason 1 Chronicles would be read after the books of Samuel, 2 Chronicles after the books of the Kings, and the writings of the Prophets would be considered in sequential order. First Jonah and Obadiah, who

lived under Ahab and Jeroboam, Kings of Israel. Second, Isaiah, Hosea, Joel, Amos and Micah, who became famous under Josiah and Hezekiah, Kings of Judah, at the time of the migration of the ten tribes. Third, Nahum and Habakkuk, who followed not long after under Manasseh. These two Prophets would then follow the others in reading just as they also follow them in time. Fourth, Jeremiah and Zephaniah, who prophesied at the time of the migration. After them, in the fifth place, Ezekiel and Daniel, who prophesied in the midst of the captivity. Finally, in sixth place, Haggai, Zechariah, and Malachi, who discharged their Prophetic office after the return from the Babylonian captivity. But it is best to observe in one's reading the order in which we find the sacred books arranged in the Bible, so as not to disrupt the memory.

(5) *The object.* For this cursory reading of the Bible, the Latin and German translations can be used alternately, one after the other, namely, in this way: First the whole German Bible is read through, then also the Latin. For both translations should be familiar to the student of theology, the German on account of its use in sermons, the Latin on account of its use in disputations. But those who are already involved in ecclesiastical ministry can use the German version alone in cursory reading.

(6) Among the various German paraphrases of the (New Testament) Bible—those of Tigurinus, Leon Judas, Piscator, Dietenberger, Emser, Polanus—only Dr. Luther's should be commended as the ordinary material for this cursory reading, of course. Not only is it alone used in the sermons that are preached to the people, but it also observes the terse character of the German language, wholly corresponds to the sense of the Hebrew text, and is able to take the place of many commentaries, which that most pious Prince George of

Anhalt (in *commen. Psa. 16.*) most highly commends. Sturmius (*de exercit. Rhetoric. ad Philippum Comitem Lippianum* pag. 8. fac. 1.):"Does not Luther stand out as the Teacher of our language, whether you consider the purity or the abundance? The counsels of princes, the judgments of states, all scribes, all legates and Christian Germans grant the man this honor as a theologian. If there were no reinstatement of this religion, if none of his sermons existed, if he had written nothing other than those things which he published in translation of the Old and New Testaments, nevertheless he would still be owed the highest and perpetual praise in this labor. For if the other translations of the Greeks, Latins and others are compared with his German translation, they will be forced to yield by the clarity, purity, propriety, and similarity to the original Hebrew. I believe that, as no painter is considered to have surpassed Apelles, so no writer will ever be able to overcome Luther's translation." Indeed, just as every year* a festival day was celebrated in the place where the translation of the LXX interpreters appeared, in memory of such a great achievement, so also Bugenhagen, with his domestic Church, held a festival on that day when Luther put the finishing touch on his German translation. Heshusius does not hesitate to place Luther's translation ahead of that Old Testament translation of the LXX interpreters.

(7) Of the various Latin versions that are extant—of Pagnini, Montanus, Vatablus, Castellio, Münster, Tremelius, etc.—the Latin Vulgate of Erasmus is to be preferred, which used to be attributed to Jerome; namely, the one that Osiander published with corrections, in which most things are referred back to the original, and in the margin an explanation of some of the more difficult passages is added.

---

*   as Philo relates in his book on the life of Moses

(8) *Manner.* In this cursory reading, it is remarkably helpful for the memory if one notes in the margin a brief summary of each chapter with as few words as possible. Thus, in the first chapter of Genesis, 'Creation' should be written in the margin. In chapter 2: 'Institution of marriage.' Chapter 3: 'Fall.' Chapter 4: 'Fratricide.' Chapter 5: 'Lives of the Patriarchs.' Chapter 6: 'Ark.' Chapter 7: 'Flood.' Chapter 8: 'Exiting the ark.' Chapter 9: 'Rainbow: Noah's drunkenness.' Chapter 10: 'Noah's posterity.' Chapter 11: 'Tower of Babel, half genealogy.' Chapter 12: 'Call of Abraham.' Chapter 13: 'Separation of Abraham and Lot.' Chapter 14: 'Abraham's victory, blessing of Melchizedek.' Chapter 15: 'Abraham's justification and sacrifice.' Chapter 16: 'Hagar and Ishmael.' Chapter 17: 'Circumcision.' Chapter 18: 'Abraham's three guests.' Chapter 19: "Destruction of Sodom.' Chapter 20: 'Abduction of Sarah.' Chapter 21: 'Birth of Isaac, Ishmael's expulsion, Abraham's covenant with Abimelech.' Chapter 22: 'Sacrifice of Isaac.' Chapter 23: 'Death and burial of Sarah.' Chapter 24: 'Marriage of Rebecca.' Chapter 25: 'Abraham's second wedding, birth of Esau and Jacob.' Chapter 26: 'Isaac's exile, covenant with Abimelech.' Chapter 27: 'Blessing of Jacob.' Chapter 28: 'Jacob's ladder.' Chapter 29: 'Jacob's wedding.' Chapter 30: "Jacob's offspring and riches.' Chapter 31: 'Jacob's return to his country.' Chapter 32: 'Jacob's struggle with Angel.' Chapter 33: 'Reconciliation of Jacob and Esau.' Chapter 34: 'Rape of Dinah.' Chapter 35: 'Rachel's death, Ruben's incest.' Chapter 36: 'Esau's genealogy.' Chapter 37: 'Selling of Joseph.' Chapter 38: 'Incest of Tamar.' Chapter 39: 'Joseph's prison.' Chapter 40: 'Dreams of cupbearer & baker.' Chapter 41: 'Joseph's exaltation.' Chapter 42: 'Arrival of Joseph's brothers.' Chapter 43: 'Arrival of Benjamin.' Chapter 44: 'Accusation of Joseph's brothers.' Chapter 45: 'Recognition of Joseph.' Chapter 46: 'Jacob's entrance into Egypt.' Chapter 47: 'Awful famine

in Egypt.' Chapter 48: 'Blessing of Ephraim and Manasseh.' Chapter 49: 'Jacob's prophecy & death.' Chapter 50: 'Burial of Jacob, death of Joseph.'

The same should be done in the rest of the chapters of the books of the Old and New Testaments, so that, after each chapter has been read through, a brief summary of it may be noted in the margin.

(9) The more notable passages should be underlined and repeated several times at the end of each reading that they may stick in one's memory.

CHAPTER 4.

THE ACCURATE READING OF SCRIPTURE.

With the term 'accurate reading,' I understand that which accurately observes and precisely records in a special notebook the connection of the members, the emphasis of the words and phrases, yes, every single thing that is worthy of note in any chapter of Scripture, after first consulting the fountains; namely, the Hebrew text in the Old Testament and the Greek in the New, as well as the translations. Four volumes of clean paper should be bound together into books. Two of them should be assigned to the books of the Old Testament, and two to the books of the New Testament. A distribution of pages should be made according to the order of Bible books and chapters, namely, in such a way that in the title area of each page the book name and chapter number are assigned, and to each Bible chapter, depending on the length and content of material, two, three, four, five, or even six pages should be set aside. It does not appear to be worth the effort to add immediately an enumeration of every single verse, since the things to be recorded in this book do not occur in every single verse. Nevertheless, a general distribution of verses can be made for every five, ten, or twenty verses, etc. Anything that comes to mind either in the accurate reading of the Bible or even in the reading of other theological writers should be recorded in this book, composed in such a way that they can be related to any of the following points.

(1) The summary and aim of any chapter. (2) Its general division. (3) The unique emphases of the words and phrases. (4) Different interpretations of the Fathers and of the more recent doctors of the Church. (5) The solutions for apparent contradictions. (6) Unique doctrines and observations, namely, things that do not come to mind at first glance, but favor some deeper investigation. (7) The strong statements of the Fathers. Anyone who notes down these seven points on a given chapter of the Bible, or has them noted down, will collect for himself a splendid treasury of theological education and will be equipped with an invaluable tool for preparing sermons and disputations. But let no one imagine that he is able in one or two or three years to fully and perfectly collect and annotate all the things in each and every Bible chapter that pertain to these seven points. No, this task extends throughout the whole course of theological study—indeed, through the whole course of a man's life. It is sufficient, then, only to note certain things the first time and to leave some empty space for the rest, so that he may be immediately able to add to this treasury the pertinent things which may occur to him in further Bible reading, or in considering other writers, or as he is listening to lectures and disputations. If someone considers taking up this Bible reading in the first or in the following years of his theological study, he should begin with the New Testament books, and then add the annotations of Camerarius, Beza, and Erasmus; the observations of Piscator of Herborn, Casaubonus, Drusius; the commentary of Flacius, Osiander, etc.; and he should diligently write down the things that seem relevant in any chapter to something under the points stated above. In the Old Testament, he should con-

sult the annotations of Münster, Mercerus, Borrhaus, and Piscator; the commentaries of Fagius for the Chaldaic paraphrase and of others who diligently weigh the emphasis of the words and phrases in the Hebrew text. As time progresses, namely, in the years that follow, but especially when a person is already installed in his office, he can add the reading of those interpreters who chose to illustrate some book of Scripture with lengthy commentaries. Lyranus, Brentius, Osiander, Piscator, and Luther, who is to be preferred to all others, wrote commentaries on all the books of the whole Scripture. Luther, Gesner, Rungius, and Lyserus wrote exceptional commentaries on Genesis; Chytraeus, Pelargus, and Ferus on all the books of Moses; Baldwin and Lavater on Joshua; Baldwin and Peter Martyr on Judges; Baldwin and Drusius on Ruth; Jerome Weller, Francis Lambert, and Peter Martyr on the books of Samuel; Martyr and Wolffius on the books of Kings; Sarcerius and Lavater on the books of Chronicles; Wolffius, Ferus, and Sacerius on Ezra and Nehemiah; Mercerus, Lavater, John de Pineda on Job; Gesner, Selnecker, Mörlin, Marloratus, Musculus, Jansenius on the Psalter; Mercerus, Dranoites, Osorius on Proverbs; Bucer, Jansenius, Lorinus on Ecclesiastes; Francis Lambert and Peresius on Song of Solomon; Pappus, Wigand, Winckelmann, Maldonatus, Christopher a Castro on the Prophets; Schnepfius and Sainctius on Isaiah; Hunnius, Aretius, Flacius, Salmeron, Marloratus on the New Testament; Chemnitz, Barradius, Jansenius, Maldonatus, and Musculus on the Gospels; Heshusius, Mylius, Rungius, Baldwin, Paraeus, etc. on the Pauline Epistles; Chytraeus, Winckelmann, Hoë, Blasius de Viega, and Paraeus on Revelation. The *Bibliotheca Theologica* of Bolduan, published in Jena in 1614, should be consulted, containing the *Elenchus Scriptorum Ecclesiasticorum*, the writings of those who commented on the sacred books of the Bible from the birth of Christ up until the year 1614; also the *Catalogus Catalogorum* of Draudius, the *Bibliotheca* of Pelargus, etc. One, or at most two, of these should be chosen when some book of the Bible is again taken up for an accurate read-through. But such a commentary should be selected that is adapted to each one's capacity and progress and that pursues a reliable explanation of the text rather than a lengthy and detailed treatment of topics and doctrines. For this purpose, Chemnitz' *Harmonia Evangelica* is highly commended as the most worthy of all to be read.

Chapter 5.

The synoptic knowledge of the Theological topics.

It is exceedingly beneficial right away in the first year of theological study to learn a certain embodiment and synopsis of the entire heavenly doctrine from certain books of methods (this is catechetical theology), to engrave it deeply in the mind, to embrace it with the memory, and to carry it around in one's mind at all times, so that a person can relate anything that later comes to mind in the whole course of theological study to the proper seat and its proper place, as it were. For this purpose, Dr. Chemnitz' *Enchiridion*, Dr. Mentzer's *Repetitio Locorum Chemnitiana*, and Hafenreffer's *Loci Theologici*, etc., can serve well. If a person has already engaged in this task in previous years, before his death, and, together with the study of languages and the arts, has embraced such a synopsis in his mind, he should advance immediately to the more accurate treatment of theological topics, which we will discuss in the study of the following year. But it should not seem bothersome to anyone to fix in the mind the principal definitions and the testimonies of Scripture joined to them, as well as the decisions of controversial questions with the supporting arguments attached. In fact, it will be of great assistance to anyone in examinations, in extemporaneous dissertations, in disputations, and sermons, and even throughout one's life, so that he does not go wandering about as in an unknown forest, but, like an attentive little bee, he will know how to bring everything into his little cell, of which we will have more to say later on.

CHAPTER 6.

ATTENDING LECTURES AND DISPUTATIONS.

We do not yet in this first year lead the student of theology down into that wrestling arena of disputations so that he should take on the role either of the Defendant or of the Opponent. Nevertheless, we encourage him to be a frequent attendee at theological disputations (if indeed they are established in the way which we will afterwards prescribe) so that he may obtain the confirmation and illustration of those things which daily occur to him in his private repetition of the theological topics. But above all we commend to him especially the frequent and diligent attendance at public lectures, and we seriously dissuade him from holding them in contempt.

(1) God has promised grace, blessing and the efficacy of the Holy Spirit to the pious gatherings that have been instituted in the churches and schools (Exo. 20:24; Mat. 18:20; Heb. 10:25).

(2) The examples of the saints in the Old and New Testaments bear witness that the information passed on from the living voice was, indeed, highly commended to the future ministers of the Church. With the living voice, the Patriarchs passed on to their successors the chief points of heavenly doctrine, which, of course, had not yet been written down in books.

(Luther on Genesis:"The sermons of the Father were not written in books, but in heaven, wherefore it is called 'the time of *Thohu*,' because it was not law or books, but the living words that were passed down to posterity through the Fathers.") After the Law was written, the Prophets explained them to their disciples in the schools with the living voice, wherefore they are called the 'sons of the Prophets.' Elijah's disciple was Elisha, whom he called into his school and selected to succeed him in the Prophetic office (1 Kings 19:20). The sons of the Prophets "lived before Elisha" in Gilgal (2 Kings 4:38), that is, the Theological School was there; that is where the disciples of the Prophets spent their time, with Elisha governing and overseeing their studies. The college of Priests and Levites was nothing other than the Theological School in which the younger Levites were informed and prepared for the ecclesiastical ministry. During the Babylonian captivity, Daniel instituted a Theological School, lest the knowledge of the heavenly doctrine should perish. After the return from the Babylonian captivity, Ezra and Nehemiah also erected schools, together with the reparation of the temple. Paul sits at the feet of Gamaliel (Acts 22:3). The Apostles were instructed in the school of Christ. Pantaenus taught in the Alexandrian school, succeeded by Clement of Alexandria, whose disciple was Origen. Dionysius Alexandrinus was a hearer of Origen, and Athenodorus after him (Euseb. lib. 5. cap. 9.) In the Carthaginian school were Tertullian and Cyprian. In the Caesarian school were Origen and Gregory of Neocaesarea. In the Antiochene school was Malchio Rhetor, who refuted the Samosatene. In the Nicomedian school was Lactantius, etc. (Euseb. lib. 6. cap. 2.) So, then, the disciples who were to be put in charge of the ministry of the Church long ago were taught with the living voice by teachers in the school of Christ in a kind of perpetual succession.

(3) (in *Epist. ad Paulin.*): "The living voice has some sort of latent energy and a greater capacity to influence," says Jerome. "The living voice has a remarkable power to teach." Scaliger (Exerc. 308.): "The voice has more influence, but reading is mute and, if continued for too long, lends itself to apathy. The things that are heard are more deeply impressed through the sense of discipline, whose ministers are ears, etc." Therefore, the things that we receive by hearing cling to the memory better and more steadfastly than the things that have been acquired by reading.

(4) Those who are self-taught do not possess as much dexterity of judgment. They speak less agreeably than those who have been instructed by others in the schools. In fact, they more often cause trouble in the Church.

SECTION 2: THE SECOND YEAR OF THEOLOGICAL STUDY.

To the second year of studies we assign: (1) the continuation of Bible reading; (2) the more accurate knowledge of theological topics; (3) the beginning of theological disputations. The first part was treated broadly in the preceding section. It remains to say more about the second and third assignments.

CHAPTER 1.

THE MORE ACCURATE KNOWLEDGE OF THEOLOGICAL TOPICS.

By no means will we be satisfied with a synoptic knowledge of theological topics gained from books of methods. We must advance in this year to a more accurate and a further treatment of them.

The Fathers and the more recent writers vary widely with regard to the order of the topics:

Augustine (in *Enchirid. ad Laurent.*) practically follows the order of the Creed. For he treats: (1) Theology in general,

or of the true wisdom that has been placed in the true service of God; (2) faith, hope, and love, in which the service of
God consists; (3) the creation of the world and the causes of
good and evil; (4) Adam's sin, the fall of the evil angels, and
the free will of man; (5) Christ the Mediator and His incarnation; (6) regeneration; (7) original and actual sin; (8) the
Baptism of John; (9) the resurrection and ascension of Christ;
(10) the Last Judgment; (11) the Holy Spirit; (12) the Church;
(13) the good angels and our reconciliation with them; (14) the
remission of sins; (15) whether purgatory exists; (16) alms; (17)
various kinds of sins and public penance; (18) the sin against
the Holy Spirit; (19) the resurrection of the flesh; (20) eternal life;
(21) God's omnipotence; (22) grace and the predestination of the
saints; (23) the will of God; (24) the foreknowledge of God;
(25) human will; (26) the state of souls after death; (27) the
Lord's Prayer; (28) love; (29) Baptism.

Damascene, in the books about the faith, treats: (1) Holy
Scripture; (2) God and His attributes / the Trinity; (3) creation and the angels; (4) the visible creation; (5) Paradise and
man; (6) God's providence, foreknowledge, predestination; (7) the
restoration of man through Christ; (8) Christ's incarnation,
death, descent into hell, ascension; (9) faith and Baptism; (10) the Eu-
charist; (11) the Antichrist; (12) the resurrection of the dead
and eternal life.

But we are not as concerned, at this point, with the order of theological topics as we are with the method to be used
in acquiring an accurate knowledge of each topic.

The student of theology should take care that a volume
of paper be bound together. In the title area he should write
down a methodical order of theological topics, which can be

gleaned either from the compendium of Hafenrefeffer, or from the synoptic table of Dr. Menzer, or from the syntagma of Dr. Himmel, or from another methodical and orthodox writer. Afterwards, a division should be made of each individual topic and to each one certain titles should be assigned, according to the laws of the method observed by those who have diligently and abundantly expounded each topic.

For instance, the following arrangement of the article concerning Holy Scripture can be made: (1) Homonymy, for the Sacred Scriptures use a word in various ways. (2) Etymology, why it is called 'sacred.' (3) Synonymy, which titles, periphrases, and praises are ascribed to Scripture both by the Biblical and by the Ecclesiastical writers. (4) Whether there is any real difference between Scripture and the Word of God. (5) The canonical books and the Apocrypha of the Old and New Testaments, both in general and in particular. (6) The Author of Scripture, which is God, where the diverse modes of divine revelation should be discussed. (7) The authority of Scripture, which it obtains from God, where the questions of whether the Scripture has its authority from the Church, or whether the Scripture has more authority than the Church, are explained. (8) The efficacy of Scripture, where one should dispute against the Schwenkfeldians, who call it 'a dead letter.' (9) The perfection of Scripture, where one should speak against traditions. (10) The perspicuity of Scripture. (11) The standard and judge of controversies, whether this dignity should be ascribed to Scripture. (12) The interpretation of Scripture, where the rules of sound interpretation are to be gathered. (13) The reading of Scripture, which applies also to the laity. (14) The translations of the Scriptures. (15) The authentic edition of the Scripture. (16) The division of the books of the Bible. (17) The definition of Scripture, which is a sort of symperasma encompassing all the preceding points. (18) The use of this topic.

The following arrangement of the article concerning God can be used: (1) The *homonymy* of this word. (2) Etymology. (3) The names attributed to the true God in Scripture. (4) Whether God exists, where the natural knowledge of God should be treated. (5) The unity of the divine essence against the polytheism of the Gentiles, the errors of the Manichaeans, of the Marcionites, etc. (6) The essential attributes of God in general and in particular. (7) The plurality of persons, where certain types of statements should be noted from which that plurality is deduced. (8) The Trinity of Persons, where one should treat the distinction of Persons, what kind of a distinction it is, where it originates, etc. (9) God the Father, His true Divinity; His personal character and the distinction from the other persons should be explained. (10) God the Son, concerning whom the same things should be proved: His true divinity from His divine names, attributes, works, and worship. (11) The Holy Spirit, concerning whom the same things are to be demonstrated, or more properly, a special topic should be established concerning the Son and the Holy Spirit. (12) The divine will. (13) Divine works, where all the works of God are related to the chief headings, namely, to the creation of all things and the restoration of the human race, and thus a foundation is laid for the divisions of the following topics. (14) The definitions of God. (15) The use of the topic concerning God.

One should proceed with the same order in the rest of the topics, according to the patterns observed by the methodical writers.

Furthermore, since the matter itself attests that, in any topic, there is a wide range of theological issues, it seems more helpful to draw the controversial questions against the Papists, Calvinists, and Photinians into a special notebook and to note in this volume the didactic portions and the controversies which were stirred up by ancient heretics and that today have been laid to rest, since they do not require as broad and as accurate a treatment as the controversies which are still being stirred up vehemently with more recent adversaries. Among these I also include those which were stirred up at an earlier time with the Schwenkfeldians, Majorists, and other heretics of smaller tribes or that are still being stirred up today, which likewise can be drawn into that didactic notebook. But the more serious and larger controversies in which one strives with the Papists, Calvinists, and Photinians should only be noted with a few words, so that it may be understood under which title they belong. The further treatment of them will be pushed back to another volume (the disposition of which will be explained later). (For the one whose purpose is to instruct the people in sermons but not to descend into the arena of disputations with the adversaries, he can write all these things down together. But the one who desires an accurate knowledge of the controversies should separate them from the didactic portions.) But to everyone who desires this accurate knowledge of theological topics we commend above all the *Loci Theologici* of Dr. Chemnitz, that he should diligently read them and convert them into sap and blood. The disputations of Lobeck on the Augsburg Confession and of Gesner and Hutter on the Formula of Concord; the Leipzig and Giessen disputations, of Schilter on the Catechism; the disputations of Heerbrand and Gerlach, of Baldwin on the Visitation Articles and the Smalcald Articles; the disputations of Forster on the Catechism,

and especially the scholarly writings of Dr. Hunnius, Dr. Menzer, Dr. Meisner and others by which the articles of Christian
doctrine are explained. If a person wanted to make a compendium of works, he could choose a certain orthodox, methodical
writer who has treated all the topics and, for each page of clean
paper inserted by the book manufacturer, note down on it the
things from the other writers that seem to have been left out by
him.

CHAPTER 2.

THE UTILITY OF THEOLOGICAL DISPUTATIONS.

Exercises in scholastic disputation are very useful and promote in no small way the studies of those who are learning. (There are two kinds of theological disputations: some are sheltered and scholastic, while others are serious, designed to be held with the adversaries themselves. The former serve as the prelude to the latter. It is of the former that we will treat here.) (1) For they provide both for an investigation into the truth and for the confirmation of it. Pico della Mirandola calls them the 'sieve of truth.' Scaliger (exerc. 308.): "As fire is made by striking stones together, so the truth is elicited from debates." (2) They are *prophylactic and alexipharmic* against the depraved opinions which are drawn, either from the writings of the heterodox or from interaction with them. (3) They remove the little stones of doubt that become lodged in the soul and shape one's judgment concerning the gravest matters. Boëtius (lib. 1. pros. 1): "Then is the mark of truth more clearly learned, when the eye is turned to the opposite of it." (4) They prepare students, so that those who have been promoted to the ecclesiastical ministries are not only "apt to teach," but also able to "rebuke those who contradict" (Tit. 1:9), "warriors for the truth and conquerors of errors," as Augustine says (lib. 4. *de doctrina Christ.* cap. 4.), "defenders of the right faith and subduers of false dogmas." (Scripture is useful, not only for teaching, but also for rebuking [2 Tim. 3:16. Neh. 4:17]. Initial skirmishes are required for waging war.) (5) The things which have been observed in private home study are put to use. (6) They sharpen the wit and render it quicker. (7) They make for a ready ability to discuss sacred matters and instruct students to be "ready to give a defense to the one who seeks a reason for the hope that is in us" (1 Pet. 3:15). (8) They shape one's character while freeing the mind from the disease of self-love and from the conceit of wisdom. They make a person accustomed to homiletical virtues, to curbing a hot temper, to restraint in controlling his gestures. (9) They show the way to explaining the more difficult passages of Scripture and to reconciling apparently contradictory passages. Disputations of this kind were initiated and consecrated by Christ, who, at the age of twelve, sat in the midst of the doctors, listening to them and asking them questions (Luke 2:47). Such disputations were repeated often among the piously educated for the perpetual benefit of the Church. (Justin Martyr disputed with Trypho, Athanasius with Arius, Basil with Photinus. They prepared themselves in the schools for those serious disputations with their adversaries by means of those famous fore-exercises[*]. Augustine attests [ep. 119. *ad Januar.*]:"In the ancient Church, disputations concerning sacred matters, as well as lectures, were also religiously held with great reverence.")

---

[*]   *progymnasmata*

CHAPTER 3.

THE MANNER AND RULES FOR DISPUTING THEOLOGICALLY AND SCHOLASTICALLY.

Theological disputations should only be approved, and they only achieve their goal, if they conform to the following rules, of which some are *general* and some are *special*.

The *general rules* concerning each debater, the defendant as well as the opponent, are these:

(1) Theological disputations should not be approached without first offering serious prayers to God, by which the illumination of the mind by the Spirit, the fashioning of the tongue and the direction of all actions are petitioned for the glory of the divine name. Disputations should also be completed with pious thanksgiving and with serious prayer that the truth, which has been confirmed and illustrated, may be sealed in the minds of the hearers. Nazianzus (in *orat. de fuga*): "The best practice of every beginning and word and deed comes from God and rests upon God."

(2) One should dispute holy matters in a holy manner, in the true fear of God and humble reverence, not as if in a theater of men, but as in the sight of God and the holy angels, yes, in the midst of the assembly of the entire Church. To dispute

without the fear of God is to subvert the truth, as Chrysostom says.

(3) Proper seriousness, therefore, should be observed as the lofty mysteries of the faith are discussed. Nothing should be done in sport; nothing should be proffered thoughtlessly.

(4) Sophistications unworthy of theological order should be banned. The love of truth should be displayed on both sides, and the laws of debate should be observed well. Even if it holds true in other types of disputation, that common proverb has no place in theological disputation: "One must deal with Sophists sophistically." Augustine (lib. 2. *de doctrina Christ.* c. 3.): "There one must guard against the desire for brawling and against any sort of childish show of deceiving one's adversary." Basil, in his epistle: "One should inquire without a desire for contention. One should respond without ill-temper and disdain. One should learn without shame and disgrace. One should teach without envy." Jerome (lib. 1. *adv. Pelag.*): "Not victory, but truth should be sought." Nazianzus (*orat. de pacc.*) says that one should debate "dogmatically, not analogically; in the way of fishermen, not in the way of Aristotle; spiritually, not wickedly; as in a Church, not in the marketplace; profitably, not ostentatiously."

(5) Jeers, taunts, and insults should be absent, which are indications of an immodest and intemperate spirit. "Reprove and be reproved," as that saying of Aristophanes goes. "It is not fitting to revile one another, as bread-barterers." Augustine (libr. 3. *contra literas Petiliani* cap. 1.) commends to us his own example in this area: "When I respond to anyone, either in person or in writing, even if I have been provoked with insulting accusations, as much as the Lord grants me, I look after

the hearer or reader, restraining and holding the thorns of vain indignation in check. I do not attempt to make myself superior to the man who insults me. Instead, I seek to help him by refuting his errors."

(6) One must also watch out for inane logomachy and striving over words. 2 Tim. 2:14: "Do not strive about words, for it is profitable for nothing except for ruining those who hear."

(7) One should abstain from untimely interruptions in which the one prevents the other from fully and clearly understanding his point. Quite often this results in pious conferences being turned into brawls and thunderous shouts.

(8) One should dispute those questions that are useful to know, necessary to understand, and defined in the Holy Scriptures. (Gregory Nazianzus [ad Eunom.] answers the question of what matters should be disputed and how far. "Only those which the sharpness of the human mind can grasp and insofar as the condition and ability of the hearer can understand. For as a too-loud voice to the ears, as too much food to the body, as too-heavy burdens to those who bear them, as too-heavy rains are harmful to the earth, so also hearers who are overwhelmed and worn out by questions that are too high and too heavy, suffer loss.") The Scholastics have also trespassed against this rule, who have dragged their vain and unnecessary questions into the Church and schools. Erasmus lists some of these (in annotat. 1. Tim. 1.): "Could God command something evil, even the hatred of Himself? Could He forbid all that is good, even the love and worship of Himself? Could He have made this world better than He made it, even from eternity? Could He form a man who could not sin in any way? Could

He reveal to anyone His own sin or condemnation? Can the propositions, 'God is a beetle' and 'God is a gourd,' be as possible as, 'God is a man,' etc.?" These are the things the Apostle is talking about in 1 Tim. 1:4, that "they cause disputes rather than the godly edification which is in faith." He also pronounces sentence against such debaters in 1 Tim. 6:4: "If anyone does not consent to the sound words of Christ and to that doctrine which is in accord with piety, he is proud, he is blinded, knowing nothing, but is obsessed with questions and disputes over words, from which come envy, contentions, blasphemies, evil suspicions, etc." "What need is there," asks Augustine (in *Enchir. ad Laurent.* cap. 59.), "that those things be affirmed or denied or necessarily defined which are unnecessary to know?" And he says (lib. 8. *de Genes. ad lit.* cap. 5.): "It is better to doubt what is hidden than to litigate what is uncertain." That famous saying of Prosperus agrees with this (lib. 1. *de vocat. gent.* cap. 7.): "The things which God has wanted to be hidden are not be investigated, but the things which He has made manifest are not to be denied, lest we be found illicitly curious in the former or damnably ungrateful in the latter." Alciatus used to say (*Suscit. princ.* lib. 1. cap. 1.) that "those useless speculations and questions can accomplish in divine worship what a dog can accomplish in a bath." I would also refer here to that saying of Drusius (in *appendice praeteritorum ad N.T. in 2. Pet. 2:22*): "The dog returns to his vomit who now returns and reintroduces Scholastic Theology into the academies. He takes that bread which proceeds from the mouth of God alone and mixes it with the leaven of the philosophers. These men convert the simplicity of believing into the curiosity and subtlety of disputing as they daily come up with new questions, most of which are useless and unknown to the Prophets and Apostles of long ago."

(9) Things which are openly blasphemous, insolent and giving occasion for offense should not be permitted in disputations. Plato (2. *de Republ.*), in his own city, did not wish to permit the statement, "God is the author of sins," either "to be uttered in jest or to be defended for the sake of practice." And elsewhere he commands: "Just as a monster's offspring should not be educated, so monstrous disputations and opinions should not be considered in the Republic." (Cic. 2. *de N. D.*) "It is an evil and wicked custom to dispute against God, whether it be done seriously or whether it be feigned."

(10) It is not fitting to dispute sacred matters topically, probably, and in both parts, but scientifically, apodictically and epistemonically, lest the academic *epoché* be introduced into theology. Augustine (libr. 10. *de civ. Dei* cap. 18.): "The city of God recoils in the face of doubt as it recoils in the face of madness." The Scholastics have hardly been mindful of this precept. With their topical arguments, they have called into doubt even those things which are of the most immovable and certain truth. The Papists and Photinians also trespass against this rule, who, as is apparent from the disputations of Bellarmine and Socinus, do not ask how the Scripture should be understood in the controversial passages, but how it can be twisted into various foreign senses.

(11) We can only discuss sacred matters apodictically if we make arguments from the proper principle of theology, namely, from the Holy Scriptures. Augustine (in *Psal. 118*): "Disputations are beneficial only if nothing but the ways of the Lord are considered there." Philosophy does not supply the subject matters to the theologian, but shows how to treat them and to discuss them. Therefore, one must beware of that dan-

gerous change to another genre*, by which the poorly formed, or at least poorly applied, philosophical axioms are set against express and clear statements of Scripture in the lofty mysteries of the faith. The chief goal and aim of theological disputations should be the vindication of the sayings of Scripture from the corruptions of the adversaries, to search for and to confirm the truth from the fountains themselves, namely, from the Holy Scriptures. For it is the character of Scripture alone to make the spirit of the Christian immovable and immutable.

These things have been said concerning the *general* rules of debate. There are two *special* rules: those that concern the *opponent* and those that concern the *defendant*.

These rules should particularly be kept before the eyes of the opponent:

(1) The opponent should direct all things to seeking the truth, which he should have as his sole purpose. Therefore, he should by no means assume the role of opponent from a desire to contradict, but from a love for seeking the truth. Thomas (22. v. 10. art. 7.): "If anyone disputes as one who doubts the faith and does not suppose the truth of the faith to be certain, but is inclined to put it to the test with his arguments, he undoubtedly sins as one who is doubtful in the faith and unbelieving. But if someone disputes the faith for the purpose of refuting errors, or even for practice, it is laudable."

(2) He should put forth his arguments peacefully and calmly. The Apostle requires the minister of the Church to show a certain peaceful calmness in serious disputations against his adversaries. So much more is this required of the Candidate of Theology in skirmishes and in those prepara-

---

*   μετάβασις εἰς ἄλλο γένος

tory exercises of disputations. 2 Tim. 2:24–25:"It is not proper for the servant of the Lord to quarrel, but to be gentle toward all, able to teach, patient, in meekness instructing those who oppose him." Augustine (in *epist. 174. ad Pascent.*):"As much as we are able, let us discuss the Holy Scriptures peaceably, without contention, not eager to vanquish one another with inane and childish animosity, in order that the peace of Christ may rather conquer in our hearts." The opponent should beware of φιλονεικία, of a love for contention, nor should he be shamefully slow to let himself be vanquished by the truth."It is better to be vanquished by one who speaks the truth than to vanquish a liar," as Sixtus used to say (in *Enchir. mor.*). In those pious and peaceful conferences, the one who concedes to the other who speaks more accurately should not be labeled 'vanquished.' That title is foreign to this affair; it should be left to field soldiers, for this is not a fight, but a friendly conversation concerned with eliciting the truth. In other contests, a sole victor obtains the prize. But in this sacred conflict, he who is vanquished by the truth, as long as he acknowledges that he has been vanquished by it, is simultaneously crowned together with the victor. It is better to be vanquished by the truth than to wish to vanquish the truth with falsehood.

(3) He must take great care lest he stray from the aim of the question that he has prepared to attack and be caught shooting aimlessly. Thus, if the status of the controversy does not seem to be satisfactorily developed, he should declare or repeat it briefly before setting forth his argument.

(4) He should flee from lengthy rhetorical discourses and flowery words, and he should reduce his arguments into a syllogistic circle. If it sometimes becomes necessary to employ some further explanation, it should only involve a summary

of the statements, made with a brief syllogism. But a syllogistic format cannot always be used, especially if our proposition depends on clear testimonies of Scripture. Christ Himself and the Apostles are the pattern. Pistorius (in *colloq. Badensi* p. 27. and 279.) judged that a clear testimony of Holy Scripture (1 Cor. 11:19) did not have the force of proof until it had been redacted into the form of a syllogism. Eusebius refers to this (libr. 5. *Hist. Eccles.* cap. 25. p. 74. edit. Basil.) concerning the followers of the heresy of Artemo (which Samosatene renewed): "They did not seek what the divine Scriptures say, but zealously trained themselves to find a syllogism with which to attack the divinity of Christ. And if anyone proposed to them a word of divine Scripture, they asked whether he might put it in the form of a connected or separate syllogism."

(5) Let him build his premises with the testimonies of Scripture, lest they appear unarmed and naked and be immediately repudiated through simple denial. If, however, any of the premises has been conceded by both sides, then one should not spend too much time confirming it.

(6) If he wants to include more members in a syllogism, he should arrange them in a particular order, namely, having presented those things on which the knowledge and proof of the rest depend. But it is better to propose each argument by itself than to accumulate many at the same time, for thus it happens that certain things are left out by the defendant and remain intact.

(7) He should use plain, clear speech that is consistent with the phrases received in the Church.

(8) If the defenses given are true and sufficient, he should happily acquiesce. But if there appears to be something to be

desired in them, he should calmly urge and confirm his thesis with earnestness or with a new argument. (The opponents should distribute among themselves the questions proposed for disputation, so that there may be an opportunity to discuss everything.)

Let the defendant set forth the following canons for himself:

(1) He should grant the opponent the whole space for presenting his argument. He should listen to the proof of the premises, not interrupt his speech, not be quick to a solution, but should first weigh carefully the members of the argument.

(2) He should take up the whole argument of the opponent, and he should not insidiously hide its most powerful strength and vigor, nor should he change his opponent's thought. Indeed, he should repeat, as much as possible, the very words of the opponent.

(3) In the examination of the opposing argument, before everything else he should weigh the conclusion to see whether it hits the mark, whether it directly opposes the thesis set forth for disputation, or whether it is foreign to the status of the question. If the latter is observed, he should simply reject the whole argument.

(4) If the former happens, that is, if the argument hits its mark, let him weigh the form of the argument to see whether it is consistent with the rules of good consequence. If a defect is revealed in form, he can reject the whole argument and ask the opponent to reduce it to a legitimate form.

(5) If the form is determined to be correct, then each individual premise should be considered. Is it true or false?

And if true, is it stated *simpliciter*, or only *secundum quid*? Is it proper or ambiguous, etc.? Then it will be readily apparent whether one should respond by denial, or by distinction, or by limitation.

(6) If the premises are rightly explained and declared, he should seek the force for his defense from the Holy Scriptures and the matter itself should be declared further from the analogy of faith and from parallel passages of Scripture. Origen (*hom. 1. in Jerem.*): "It is necessary for us to call on the Holy Scriptures to testify, for our senses and our expositions are not reliable apart from these witnesses."

(7) If some statement of Scripture is brought in by the opponent, the foundations should be inspected, the aim of the entire chapter must be attended, the order and connection should be considered, the things that come before and the things that come after. He must compare them with similar passages, etc., so that he may get at the true and genuine sense of that statement.

(8) If they introduce the testimonies of the Fathers or of more recent writers who are otherwise orthodox, one should consider first whether they are opposed to the thesis that has been presented, or whether their statements can be understood in a good sense first, before immediately and thoroughly rejecting them with an attack. If not, Augustine's statement should be calmly repeated (lib. 2. *contra Crescon. Grammat.* cap. 23.): "Let us use that freedom to which the Lord has called us. And of those men whose praises we shall never equal, with whose many letters our own writings cannot be compared, whose skill we cherish, in whose mouth we delight, whose love we admire, whose martyrdom we adore—if they understood something

in any other way but the canonical, let us not accept it. Nor do we do them any injury when we distinguish any writings or statements of theirs from the canonical authority of the divine Scriptures. For surely it was not without reason that the ecclesiastical Canon was established with such salubrious vigilance, to which certain books of the Prophets and Apostles belong, which we do not dare to judge in any way, and according to which we judge all other writings, both of believers and of unbelievers." And also that which still held true in the Church in the age of Thomas Aquinas (part. 1. q. 1. art. 8. ad 2.): "Of necessity, the sacred doctrine properly uses the authorities of Canonical Scripture for making an argument, while it uses the authorities of other teachers of the Church, not for proving something as from the proper authorities, but in a probable way. For our faith depends on the revelation given to the Prophets and Apostles who wrote the canonical books, not on the revelation given to the other teachers, if there was any."

(9) If a philosophical principle is introduced and it can be reasonably explained and limited so that it cannot be applied to the proposed thesis, it must first be considered that, if the opponent does not admit that explanation and limitation, he is to be called back to the proper principle of theology, namely, Holy Scripture, lest theological conferences be turned into philosophical contentions.

(10) The defendant should take great care not to allow himself to be moved to anger and not to permit his serenity of spirit to be darkened by a whirlwind of emotions, or else, through the disturbance of his mind and confusion of his judgment, an obstacle will be hurled at him so that he may not duly reflect on the sacred and august matters before him.

(11) He should bear the impoliteness of his opponent with a level and generous spirit, for it is the highest praise of wisdom to bear with the immodesty and foolishness of others.

The remaining things can be learned from the practice itself.

SECTION 3: THE THIRD YEAR OF THEOLOGICAL STUDY.

In the third year of studies, Bible reading will continue. This gives us the upper hand, as they say. The exercises in disputation will continue, which are the peculiar jewel of academic conversation. Progress will also be made in the more accurate knowledge of theological topics. But our special emphasis this year is on the controversies with the Papists, beginning with the writings of our own theologians against them. (Who can enter diseased dwellings without danger or handle poison safely, if he has not first been inoculated with an antidote?)

Some of these writings deal in general with each and every controversy that has arisen between our Church and the Papist Church, among which the following stand out: Chemnitz' *Examen Tridentinum*; Dr. Menzer's *Disputationes Antipistorianae*; Heilbrunner's *Causae recusati Concilii Tridentini, Papatus acatholicus*; the *Disputationes de plerisque controversiis cum Papatu agitatis* in the tomes of the Marburg and Giessen Disputations; Junius' observations against Bellarmine; Willetus' synopsis of Papism entitled *Capita doctrinae Jesuiticae Rupellis*; Vorstius' *Anti-Bellarminus contractus*, etc.

But other writings deal with certain controversies in particular: concerning the Scripture, the writings of Dr. Hunnius, Laur. Laelius, Whitaker, Lubertus Rainoldus, Danaeus, etc.; concerning the Church: Dr. Hunnius, Osiander, Whitaker, Lubertus, Willetus, Carletanus, Usserius, Mornaeus, etc.; concerning the councils: Gesner, Förster, Whitaker, etc.; concerning the Roman Pope and the Antichrist: Dr. Hunnius, Phil. Nicol. Balduinus, Whitaker, Lubertus, Povelus, Mornaeus' *Mysterium iniquitatis*, Sutlivius, the colloquy of Rainoldus with Hartus; concerning the image of God and original sin: Whitaker, Paraeus, Willerus; concerning free will: Dr. Hunnius; concerning justification: Dr. Battus, Carletanus; concerning the Mass: Dr. Hutter, Mornaeus; concerning marriage: Dr. Tarnovius; concerning purgatory: Sutlivius, etc.

From the writings of the Papists, the following should suffice: Bellarmine's *Commentaria*, Gregory de Valentia's *Disputationes in Thomam*, the *Enchiridion* of Costerus, Stapleton's *De principiis doctrinalibus*, Pistorius' *Hodegeticon*, Becanus' *Theologia Scholastica*. For whatever things occurs in the rest of the Papist writers are all found in these—indeed, in Bellarmine alone. Therefore, he could be the one who represents them all.

Furthermore, in order that the treatment of these controversies may be clearer and more beneficial*, progress will be made in the following way. First, all the controversies that have arisen between the Papists and us should be divided into certain classes, according to the order of theological topics provided above, or according to the order observed by Bellarmine. Under each topic, according to the laws of method, they should be arranged so that the more general things, and those things that serve for the knowledge and confirmation of the things that follow, should be placed ahead of the rest.

---

*   Aug. in *Enchirid. ad Laurent.* c. 5.: "Disputation against the heretics is a book of many chapters. Indeed, it is infinite."

Each controversy should be explained in this order: First, the true status of the controversy should be developed, where known questions, the charges of the adversaries concerning this question, and all those things which do not enter into the controversy but are conceded by both sides, should be removed. (Tertullian testifies of himself somewhere that, when he stepped forth onto the battle line of disputation, he marked off the sum of the question with certain lines, lest he should appear to wander outside the parameters of the matter at hand.)

Then two sections should be set up. The first contains the fundamental points of our opinion, divided into three or four classes.

The first class is sought from the Scriptures, to which pertain not only the express testimonies of Scripture, but also the reasonable conclusions that have been deduced from the Scriptures by legitimate consequence. For those things which are deduced from the Sacred Writings by good consequence have the same force as those things affirmed in them with express words.

The second class contains the testimonies of the Fathers, to which also pertain the decrees of the Councils.

The third class contains the consensus of some of the adversaries themselves, both ancient (namely, the Scholastics) and modern Papist writers. For we will demonstrate in its place that no controversy exists between us and the Papal Church in which we cannot, for the sake of establishing our opinion, introduce clear and evident testimonies from the adversaries themselves. This clearly demonstrates the efficacy of the truth, which even strikes eyes that have been closed. No form of proof is better at weakening the malice of the wicked than that which is drawn from the profession of the adversaries. Furthermore, no victory is judged clearer or nobler than when we win with our own enemies as judges (Deu. 32:21). See Osiander's *Papa non-papa*, Hunnius's *Labyrinthus Papisticus*, Flacius' *De sectis ac dissidiis Pontificiorum*, Mortonus' *Apologia Catholica*.

Finally, to a fourth class can be added philosophical reasons, namely, in those questions to which we can ascend by the light of Nature.

Each page should be divided into two parts, with our arguments noted on one side, and on the other, the exceptions of the adversaries that have been linked with our responses. It is not necessary to form whole syllogisms, but it is enough to write down half of it. Likewise, if the passages of Scripture are lengthy, it is sufficient to note their chapter and verse or the beginning of the passage. The primary bases and the more compelling points should be written down. Things that are more trivial or too tedious to elaborate should be judged unworthy of annotation.

The second section sets forth the arguments of the adversaries in the same way, so that on one side of a page the arguments themselves are noted in a few words, on the other side our responses[*]. If a person progresses in this order through

[*] Hilary advises (lib. 8. *de Trin.*): "We should be concerned with two things in refuting those who talk idly. First, that we teach that which is sound, holy and perfect. Our speech, as it wanders about through certain curves and bends and then emerges from remote and windy rabbit holes, should seek rather than demonstrate the truth. Secondly, the things which are adapted from those word tricks of inane and fallacious opinions to the appearance of a true flatterer, those very things we must expose as inept and absurd to the conscience of all. For it is not enough to have taught what is pious, unless by 'pious' are understood the wicked

each controversy, he will complete this task by the very end of this third year.

---

things that are also refuted."

Section 4: The fourth year of theological study.

Bible reading, exercises in disputation, and the task of more accurately understanding the topics will continue in the fourth year of studies. But there will be two unique tasks this year: (1) A thorough treatment of the controversies with the Calvinists and the Photinians. (2) The beginning of the practice of preaching sermons in the Church.

Chapter 1.

A treatment of the Calvinistic and Photinian controversies.

This treatment should be made in altogether the same manner which we suggested to be used for treating the controversies with the Papists, with one exception. The testimonies of even the most ancient Fathers are produced in vain against the Photinians; in their estimation, such testimonies are not worth a penny.

As one is about to begin a more accurate treatment of the Calvinistic controversies, he should first read our writings, some of which attack in general the entire system of Calvinistic doctrine, such as Schlüsselburg's *Theologia Calvinistica*; Heilbrunner's *Synopsis Calvinismi*; the *Refutatio orthodoxi consensus*; the disputations of Marburg and Giessen; the writings of the Württemberg and Wittenberg Theologians *Contra librum Staffordiensem*; Eckhart's *Enchiridion Controv.*; but above all, the Formula of Concord and its Apology, etc.

But other writings thoroughly treat certain controversial articles in particular. Concerning the person of Christ, the following should be read: Chemnitz' *De duabus naturis*, Hunnius, Gesner, Mentzer *Contra Sadeelem & Martinium*; Schröder's little works *De comm. proprii, De donis infinitis Christo datis, De sessione ad dextram Dei, Thronus Regalis Christi*, etc.; concerning predestination: Hunnius, Lobech, Sluterus; concerning the Supper: Chemnitz, Hunnius, Mentzer *Contra Sadeelem*, etc.

From the writings of the adversaries, the following should be read: Calvin's *Institutio*, *Orthodoxus consensus*, the *Institutiones* of Bucanus, Ursinus' *Catechesis*, the *Syntagma* of Polanus, P. Martyr's *Loci communes*, the works of Sadeel, etc.

Against the Photinians the following should be read: Zanchius' *De Natura Dei & tribus Elohim*, Wigand's *De Deo*, Grauer's *Examen praecipuarum Sophisticationum*, Mentzer's *Exegesis in August. Confess.*, Frantzius' *Disputationes in Augustanam confessionem*, Jac. Martin's *Libri duo de tribus Elohim*, Smiglecius' *De Deo Ariano*, Meisner's *Consideratio Theologiae Photinianae*, Hunnius' *Examen errorum Photinian.*, etc., and the particular disputations of other theologians of ours against those most pestilent heretics.

From the writings of the Photinians, it is sufficient to read the *Catechesin Racoviensem majorem*, Ostorodus' *Institutio-*

nes, and the writing of Socinus entitled *Quod regni Poloniae & magni Ducatus Lithuaniae homines*. These men should be joined to the company of those who, in the same places, are unjustly called Arians and Ebionites. But no one should rush blindly into reading those diabolical blasphemies that are contained in the writings of the Photinians, unless he is well instructed in the foundations of the true religion and is sufficiently fortified against them from the writings of the orthodox.

CHAPTER 2.

THE PRACTICE OF PREACHING.

Since those who are in a hurry to give sermons, even though they have not yet attained a grasp of the heavenly doctrine and their judgment has not yet been confirmed, usually fail miserably, we have chosen to postpone the practice of ecclesiastical homiletics to the fourth year of studies. Meanwhile, we prescribe nothing to those who, either endowed with singular natural ability or compelled by necessity of private property, aspire to this goal and practice of theological study more quickly. (No one should approach sermon-writing nor ascend the pulpit unless he has first offered (1) serious prayer to God that He would open his lips to declare the praise of His name and guide his heart and tongue in such a way that he does not say anything that would destroy the Word, injure the glory of God, or be an offense or a nuisance to his hearers. (2) Pious meditation, lest he should rashly and abruptly blurt out anything that enters his mouth, but that all things be recalled to the file for polishing before they are called to the tongue. For if this grave admonition of Christ applies anywhere, it certainly applies here. Matthew 12:35: "I say to you that men will render an account for every idle word on the day of judgment." Gregory Nazianzus (in orat. 39. in S. *lumina* tom. 1. p. 630. edit. Billii.): "With tongue and mind and thought I tremble, as often as I preach a word about God, which is also the splendid and blessed emotion that I have wanted to be in you." "Blessed are the lips," says Jerome (*de laud. Virg.*), "which never emit what they wish to recant.")

Furthermore, there are two duties of the ecclesiastical preacher: *the interpretation of Scripture and the adaptation of it to a salutary use.* The interpretation of Scripture involves both *the investigation of the true and genuine sense* and *the narration of the same.* For it is not enough to inquire after and track down the genuine sense of Scripture, but beyond that, it is required of the preacher that he fully recount to the people in ecclesiastical sermons the true sense that he has discovered. The former pertains to the private study of the preacher; the latter to his public office. The former has been explained in the treatise *On the Interpretation of Scripture* with regard to the tools and means by which it can be obtained; the latter remains to be explained here with regard to the manner in which it is to be accomplished.

The narration of the true sense is nothing other than a paraphrastic explanation of the text. The adaptation of the discovered and recounted sense to a salutary benefit is nothing other than the gathering of doctrines from the text and the application of them to the salvation of those who hear. Both must be joined together in sermons, since the one without the other is imperfect and unfruitful. Furthermore, as the Rhetoricians state the five duties of the orator—*discovery, arrangement, style, memory and delivery**—so also the same can be considered in the oratory of the preacher, that is, in ecclesiastical oratory. Thus, we will also outline the canons that are usefully observed in preparing and presenting sermons to the people according to these five members.

---

*   *Inventio, Dispositio, Elocutio, Memoria, Pronunciatio*

To *discovery* pertains the concern for fully treating matters in a sermon, of which this is the general canon. The matters themselves that are to be set forth in sermons should be sought from the Holy Scriptures. For they are the only and proper principle for discussing divine matters, the only salutary means for knowing God and the most certain remedy against all errors and evils. Isaiah 8:20: "to the Law and to the testimony." Luke 16:29: "they have Moses and the Prophets." John 5:39: "Search the Scriptures." 1 Peter 4:11: "He who speaks, let him speak as the utterances of God." 2 Peter 1:19: "We have the firmer prophetic word, to which you do well to attend, as to a light shining in a dark place, etc." A logical consequence of this canon is (1) that the Preacher should by no means revel in citing the sayings of the Fathers, especially among the more unlearned hearers, for there is a great difference between the sayings of the Prophets and Apostles and the testimonies of the Fathers. The writings and sayings of the former supply the solid foundation of faith (Eph. 2:20). But the latter are to be judged from the writings of the Prophets and Apostles and examined according to them. It is sufficient, therefore, with the hearers in mind, either for the sake of the consensus of witnesses or on account of pithy and emphatic brevity, to cite three or four sayings of the Fathers in a sermon, but never with the same abundance and number as the testimonies of Scripture that are introduced, since Scriptural testimonies are not to be considered in the same place together with the Fathers. Christ and the Apostles, in their sermons, seek the foundations of their doctrine from Moses and the Prophets; they certainly do not inquire at the same time into the commentaries of the Rabbis. Indeed, it can easily happen that the more unlearned begin to suspect that the same force of proof and the same weight of authority belong to the sayings of the Scripture and the Fathers, if both are indiscriminately cited with the same abundance and frequency. (2) That moral sayings of the heathens or profane stories should be cited far more sparingly (read Thomas Waley's *Moralitates in Metamorphosin Ovidianam*, and you will be amazed at the outrageous malignancy of mingling the sacred with the profane), for God never promised that He would, through these means, be efficacious for conversion and salvation in the hearts of men, but always ascribes this working of His grace solely and uniquely to His Word, as the means and instrument appointed for it by Him (Isa. 55:10; Luke 24:31; Acts 16:14; Rom. 1:16; 1 Tim. 4:16; Heb. 4:12, etc.). It should be noted, of course, that the Apostle quoted three verses from the heathen poets: the half-verse from Aratus' *Phaenomena*, "For we are also His offspring" (Acts 17:28); the iambic senarius from Menander, "Evil company corrupts good habits" (1 Cor. 15:33, concerning which verse Tertullian [lib. 1. *ad uxorem* cap. 8.] says that "He was sanctified by Paul"), and the hexameter from Epimenides, "Cretans are always liars, evil beasts, lazy gluttons" (Tit. 1:12). But he was dealing with those among whom the books of the heathens were held in high esteem—indeed, who had yet to be converted from heathenism to Christ. Not that we absolutely and simply disapprove quoting some poignant and pithy saying from the heathens, but we contend that it should be done very sparingly and sensibly. The same holds true for profane stories. If the preacher dwells on them too long, he will cause his hearers to hear the Word of the living God with a sleepy and distracted mind. Indeed, he will cause them to eagerly long for some story to be told that will charm their ears and delight their mind. The Word of God alone is "living and effective" (Heb. 4:12), is the "Word of Spirit and life" (John 6:63), is the inexhaustible fountain of divine wisdom, so that there is little need for the sayings of the heathens or for profane stories as some kind of supplement. (If at any time examples of virtues or sayings about zeal for virtue are drawn from the heathens, a comparison of unequal values should be added. We should be ashamed that the heathens surpass us in the area. Jerome says everywhere in his Epistles: "If the blue dye of the Britons[*] is worth so much, how much more that most precious pearl!" Likewise: "Let these things be said to bruise us, if faith does not surpass what unbelief has furnished.")

While these things have been said in general concerning the discovery of the things that are to be presented in sermons, it remains for us to discuss two areas of theological and homiletical discovery in particular, namely, both *the paraphrastic narration of the genuine sense* and *the adaptation of it to the benefit of the hearers*.

Narration, *with respect to the object,* is either *general* or *specific*. *General* narration is directed toward a whole book; *specific* narration, to a chapter of some book of the Bible, or to some pericope of a chapter, to which pertains the explanation of the Sunday Gospels and Epistles. In general narration, one is to explain: (1) *The canonical authority of the book.* (2) *The intermediate author,* that is, the efficient instrumental cause. (3) *The object,* namely, to whom it was written. (4) *The impulsive cause* for writing, that is, the occasion which prompted the writing itself, where one should explain what the status of the Church was at the time of writing. (5) *The subject* that is chiefly and principally treated in that writing, what the aim and principal question is. (6) *The general arrangement,* explaining the chief and principal parts of the whole writing. (7) *The utility* that one hopes to gain from it, where one should enumerate the principal passages and the chief doctrinal headings that are treated and explained in it.

---

[*]   *vitrum*

The *specific* narration of the same chapter or pericope considers and explains *the words, subject matter, and arrangement.* It is occupied with the *words* in this way, that, for the benefit of grammar, it explains from the original language the foreign expressions, the ambiguous emphases of the expressions and the idioms of the phrases; and for the benefit of Rhetoric, it declares the tropical and figurative language. It is occupied with the *subject matter* in this way, that it explains the *efficient cause*, the one who is responsible for doing or saying that which is treated in the text; the *object* to whom those things were said; *the cause because of which; the material,* that is, *the subject about whom; the circumstances of time and place,* when and where the things were said or done; *the antithesis* that opposes the words and deeds, etc. It is occupied with the *arrangement* in this way, that it expounds the principal aim, the line of argument, the connection with what comes before and what follows, and even the elegant design of the proposed text.

The canons of this paraphrastic narration are as follows.

(1) The narration should be *brief and clear,* unless obscurity requires a lengthy presentation. We do not approve, therefore, if proper and clear expressions are unnecessarily declared with many words.

(2) In narration, a comparison of both similar and dissimilar passages should be made, so that it is clear in how many ways a vocable is used in the Scriptures and what the proper meaning of the vocable is in the text. The Bible concordances that exist today in the Hebrew, Greek, Latin, and German languages are useful in fulfilling this purpose.

(3) In narration, everything in a story can be reduced to *that which precedes, that which is done,* and *that which follows.* They

can likewise be reduced to the circumstances of *persons, place, time, causes, etc.*, which shed much light on the explanation of the story.

(4) In the narration of the Old Testament, one should have in view the fulfillment in the New Testament, for the outcome is the best interpreter of prophecies.

(5) In the narration of the New Testament, the minds of the hearers should be called back to the prophecies and types of the Old Testament, for that which has been fulfilled in the New Testament was announced ahead of time and prefigured in the Old.

(6) In explaining the expressions and phrases from the original language, one must beware of all forms of ostentation, lest many things should be presented in a language that is foreign and unknown to the hearers. Instead, the unique characteristics and emphases of the expressions should be expressed in the vernacular, as much as possible.

(7) One should display propriety and discretion in removing false and strange explanations, lest all the interpretations of ancient and modern writers be introduced; only the chief interpretations should be cited, and always with a simple summary added. One form of narrating the text should be used in the schools among the educated, another in the churches before the more unlearned.

(8) If the interpretation that is introduced is opposed by some, it should be proven from the things that come before and after, from the aim, from the analogy of faith, from the comparison of passages, from the testimonies of the most ancient interpreters.

Now that these things have been said about narration, it follows that we speak about adapting the salutary exposition and narration of the text to the benefit of the hearers. Various manners of that adaptation are necessary because of the diversity and variety of hearers with whom the theologian is concerned. For some are still *unbelievers*, whose minds are to be prepared for accepting the Christian religion from a discourse solicited from the book of Nature (Acts 17:22). Some are still *unlearned*, for whom *milk* is to be prescribed, as the Apostle directed (1 Cor. 3:1, Heb. 5:13), that is, the fundamental points of Christian doctrine are to be passed on through catechetical questions. Some are *impenitent and secure*, to whom the threats of the Law are to be presented, so that the "grief that is according to God" may be stirred up in their hearts (2 Cor. 7:10). Some are bewitched with erroneous opinions; these must be more correctly informed from God's Word, and the stones of doubt must be dislodged from their minds. Some are *humble and contrite*; they must be built up by the comfort of the Gospel. Some are disturbed by *various temptations*, to despair, to pride, concerning weakness of faith, concerning perseverance, etc. To all of them, the remedy must be offered which comes from the medical office of the heavenly Word.

But since all these things have to do with individual situations and pertain more to the salutary benefit of private confession and absolution than to sermons, we shall not consider here the beneficial adaptation of Scripture in a universal, but in a special sense, as it should be done in sermons presented to the people. But since there the whole assembly of the Church is to be instructed, which consists of various and diverse people, the aim and manner of adaptation cannot be uniform, but must be multiplex, various, and diverse, which we will summarize under the following five headings, following in the footsteps of the Apostle. Romans 15:4: "Whatever things were written before were written for our instruction, that, through the patience and the comfort of the Scriptures, we might have hope." And 2 Timothy 3:16, 17: "All Scripture is inspired by God and is profitable for instruction, for reproof, for correction, for training in righteousness, that the man of God may be proficient, thoroughly equipped for every good work." From these apostolic declarations, it is gathered that there is a fivefold use of Scripture, for it serves for *instruction*, for *reproof*, for *correction*, for *training*, and for *comfort*. The basis of this fivefold use must be explained.

The Scripture was given by God to this end: that men might be educated for salvation from it (2 Tim. 3:15); that it may provide the remedy against the evil brought upon the human race through the first fall; that it may produce a pious man and a perfect Christian. But now that the human race has been powerfully subjected to a threefold malady through, and on account of, original sin, we are blind and unlearned *in knowing the truth*, slow and sluggish *in doing good*, weak and impatient *in enduring evil*. Scripture cures the first malady through *instruction*, the second through *training*, and the third through *comfort*. Not only are we blind and unlearned when it comes to knowing the truth, but we are also inclined to devise or to embrace errors. Scripture cures this malady through *reproof*. Not only are we slow and sluggish in doing good, but we are also quick and prone to doing evil. Scripture cures this malady through *correction*.

On the other hand, there are three chief works of the true Christian, namely, *to know the truth*, *to do good*, and *to endure evil*, whence also are numbered the three cardinal and chief virtues of the Christian man: faith, love and hope. To faith pertains the knowledge of the truth; to love, doing good; to hope, enduring evil. But since the knowledge of the truth does not exist without the removal of what is false, nor does doing good take place unless one retreats from evil or sin, the five aforementioned members are generally required for obtaining the perfection of Christian piety (as it applies to this life). *Instruction and reproof* have knowing the truth in view; *training and correction*, doing good; and *comfort*, the patient endurance of evil. Those who delight in dichotomies can go on in this manner.

The adaptation of Scripture is either *theoretical* or *practical*. The theoretical involves *knowing the truth*, wherefore *instruction* involves *refuting falsehood*, wherefore *reproof* ensues. The practical involves doing good, wherefore *training* involves fleeing from the evil of guilt, wherefore *comfort* ensues. (Concerning these kinds of adaptation, it should generally be noted that those passages are to be chosen from the text which are applicable to the people, times, and places where the sermon is being given.)

The canons of *instruction* are:

(1) The doctrines should not be foreign to the text, from somewhere far removed, but should flow from the text in such a way that they are either contained in it in the words themselves or are deduced from it through good and obvious consequence.

(2) The doctrine of both the Law and the Gospel should be treated in sermons. But since there are a greater number of impenitent and worldly men in that common assembly of the Church, law-sermons are more frequently to be urged and encouraged. It should be added that the salutary

benefit of the Gospel does not take place in people's hearts unless they are first crushed by the hammer of the Law.

(3) One must guard zealously against confusing the Law and the Gospel. As Luther testifies, the chief part of theological understanding consists in accurately discerning the doctrine of the Law from the Gospel. (The ministers of the Church are commanded in 2 Tim. 2:15 to "rightly divide the word of truth." If the Gospel is preached to the impenitent and secure, and the Law is left out, they are confirmed in their wickedness. If the severity of the Law is urged against those who have been crushed, and the Gospel is left out, they are driven to despair.)

(4) The doctrines which are derived from stories should be demonstrated with some clear and evident Scripture passage, for it is not proper to weave together any doctrines whatsoever out of each and every event, but one must always respect the universal and common rules.

(5) In drawing out doctrines from the effects to the cause, from the position of the one to the removal of the opposite, from the similar to the similar, etc., a course can be established. Much can be ascribed to pious meditation proceeding from a penitent and devout heart, as long as it is accompanied by the serious invocation of God and the diligent reading of Scripture.

(6) In explaining the articles of faith before the people, the necessary and fundamental points should be treated, leaving the subtle and arduous questions for the schools.

(7) When a confirming argument has been made by which some article of faith is strengthened and reinforced,

other arguments can also be brought in from other passages of Scripture, not only so that the perfect harmony of Scripture may be shown, but also in order that the minds of the hearers may be all the more confirmed in the truth.

The canons of *reproof*.

(1) Not all controversies are to be treated before the people, but only those which concern the fundamental articles of faith that are necessary to be known by all.

(2) Those things should especially be explained which are being especially stirred up in our time and which present some sort of imminent danger to our hearers. But those things which have already been treated extensively, or which seem to present no danger to our hearers—perhaps because they are not well-known—should be wrapped up in religious silence.

(3) One garners the most favor with reproof if it is clear that the occasion for refuting the errors of the adversaries is presented from the text itself, without the preacher having gone looking for it elsewhere.

(4) Errors are to be refuted with clear, fundamental testimonies of Scripture that directly and properly pertain to the question at hand.

(5) One must guard against an uncontrolled temper, outbursts, taunting expressions and all buffoonery, nor should one use harsher words than the situation demands.

(6) It does not seem beneficial for one's hearers, especially for the more unlearned, to use terms of Logic in the formation and refutation of the arguments introduced by the adversaries.

(7) One should direct neither the whole sermon nor the majority of it toward reproving errors, but should return immediately to the doctrines, exhortations, and admonitions which are more necessary for the common assembly of the Church.

The canons of *training*.

(1) There must be very frequent exhortation to zeal for piety and to the duties of the Christian man in this old world in which love is nearly dead.

(2) The stories of the saints presented in the Holy Scripture supply further material for exhortation to piety.

(3) Everything in the exhortations should be directed, not only to the external works, but also to the advancement of the inner man, which consists in putting to death the Old Adam, contempt for the world, self-denial, sincere humility of the heart, etc.

(4) In exhortations with respect to the state, condition, and vocation of the hearers, the exhortations should not be unreasonable or irrelevant. He wastes his breath who preaches in princely halls to those who are surrounded by luxury and an abundance of all things, exhorting them to endure poverty.

(5) The general rules and admonitions that occur in the Scriptures should be transferred to the specific, namely, from thesis to hypothesis, according to the Apostle's command in Romans 15:4: "Whatever things were written in the past were written for our instruction." And 1 Cor. 10:11: "These things were written for our admonition."

(6) When the Biblical forms of prayer, thanksgiving, benediction, etc., have been explained, an exhortation

should be added immediately and a paraenetic invitation to imitation.

(7) After *instruction and reproof*, some brief exhortation should always be added, so that the hearers may persevere in the truth that has been acknowledged, while fleeing from the errors that are opposed to it. Indeed, it is to that end that both instruction and reproof are treated.

The canons of *correction*.

(1) The correction of morals is particularly necessary as we live in these utterly corrupt dregs of the last age.

(2) The material for such correction is supplied, not only by the law-sermons of the Prophets and their threats of punishment, but also by the rules for living piously, prescribed in the Scriptures. For the straight is the indicator of the crooked.

(3) Indeed, everything the Scripture says about the righteousness of God has to do with kindness and truthfulness, providing an occasion for correction. For if God is just and the avenger of crimes, why are we not afraid to kindle His wrath against us with sins? If He is good and merciful, why are we not ashamed to show Him such ill favor in return for His fatherly benevolence? If He is true when He speaks, why do we not tremble at His threats?

(4) Wherever the pious are commended for deeds well done and honored with rewards, the wicked, for their part, are exposed for their sins and inflicted with punishment. Wherever God, through the Prophets, utters a complaint about the wickedness, security, and impenitence of His people, there fur-

ther material for correction is set forth. The deeds and rewards of the pious expose our negligence, that we do not walk in their footsteps, that we are not so diligently occupied with a zeal for piety, that we think little of eternal possessions, that we do not aspire to the promised rewards with all our heart. The sins and punishments of the wicked expose us, that we are not found mourning over sins in the same way; that we do not allow ourselves to be brought by so many signs of divine wrath to the intended goal; that, for the meager and momentary pleasures of the body, for worldly honor, for fleeting riches, we depart from the path of justice and piety to crooked and perverse ways. The complaints of God expose us, that we furnish Him with the same material for complaining about us.

(5) In correction, the status of the hearers and of the times must be kept in view. In vain he accuses of the haughtiness of fine clothing who preaches to the poor in the hospital. Thus, when the year's plenty overwhelms us, an occasion is provided for correction the abuse of the gifts of God.

(6) One should not rely on uncertain rumors, so that corrective sermons are preached on their account; nor should the names of any individuals be mentioned; nor should anything be presented from personal animosity; nor should great scandals be treated lightly; nor should one make tragic pronouncements in trivial matters.

(7) As Nazianzus says about the fatherly reprimands of God, "He tempers the sword of vengeance with the oil of kindness," so should the preacher act in all things, so that the hearers perceive that his reprimands proceed from a fatherly spirit and from the desire for his hearers' salvation, lest "the ministry of just correction be converted into weapons of fury."

(Gregory *homil. 18. in Evang.*) Augustine has this to say (*Epist. 64. ad Aurelium*): "Feasts are celebrated daily in honor of the martyrs. Therefore, let them be held, not harshly, to the extent that I judge, not severely, not in a domineering way, but more by teaching than by commanding, more by warning than by threatening, for thus one should deal with the multitude of sinners. If the truth is to be enforced on the sins of a few, and if we threaten anything, let it be done with grief, by threatening the coming vengeance from the Scriptures, so that, not we in our authority, but God in our speech, may be feared."

(8) Much weight is added to correction if progression is made from the lesser to the greater. There is an example of this in Romans 11:22. If they are to be gathered to the left hand of Christ who did not feed the hungry nor clothe the naked, why should they not fear who have snatched to themselves the goods of their neighbor through injustice and deceit?

The canons of *comfort*.

(1) The divine promises supply the material for comfort.

(2) Likewise, the examples of the saints, who were subject to the same adversities and, in the end, experienced divine liberation from them.

(3) The passages about God's mercy, the benefits of Christ, the joy of eternal life, etc. Bernard speaks beautifully of this (*de convers.* cap. 30.): "The sufferings of this age are not worth comparing to the past guilt that is remitted; to the present grace of comfort that is immitted; and to the future glory that is promised."

(4) The proper and frequent explanations of the reasons why the pious are subjected to the cross in this life supply further material for comfort.

(5) A comparison between the inner good things that have been granted to us by divine kindness and the external evils that we endure greatly strengthens patience.

(6) As is the rule of all true piety, so also here: In Christ, to bear up patiently against all kinds of evil is sufficient medicine. Bernard (cap. 4. *super ego vitis* col. 1602.): "It is not right for the member to be pampered under the head who is pierced with thorns."

(7) As inner temptations exercise a man more severely than external evils, so also both more frequent and more powerful comforts are to be contrasted with them.

These things have been said about the *discovery* of the matters to be set forth in sermons. Now follows the *arrangement*, concerning which the following canons are to be observed.

(1) The arrangement of the entire sermon is set up in this way. First, an introduction is presented, to which is added a brief summary of the text that is going to be explained, followed by an outline, to which is frequently added a brief prayer for obtaining the illumination of the Holy Spirit. Each part is then declared paraphrastically and adapted to the salutary benefit of the hearers in the manner already demonstrated. After all the parts have been explained in this way, a conclusion is added, repeating the summary of the sermon, ending with a pious prayer to God.

(2) The introduction should not be foreign to the text, from somewhere far removed, artificial, pompous, disjoint-

ed, or lengthy, but appropriate for the proposed text.

(3) It should arouse attention in the minds of the hearers. If one is preaching on a narration of a New Testament text, the introduction should be taken from some well-known Bible story or from a prophecy of the Old Testament, as demonstrated from the two Cherubim on the ark of the covenant, who were facing each other as they looked down upon the Mercy Seat. But how one is to deal with types and allegories and how far one is to delve into them has been explained in the treatise *On the Interpretation of Scripture*, par. 139.

(4) There should not be a steep descent from the introduction, but as if descending by steps toward the proposition.

(5) The general division should consist of two parts, or at most three.

(6) In preparing the sermon, one should not descend beyond the third subdivision, for the memory of the more unlearned is disturbed by subdivisions, and by those detailed subdivisions of subdivisions. As Seneca says, "That which is divided too much is reduced to dust."

(7) *Instruction* must always come first, and only then are the *reproof, training, correction and comfort* to be added. These are to be treated in this way, that they may be left as barbs in the minds of the hearers.

(8) Rhyming and alliteration are not altogether forbidden in the divisions, but one must take care lest anything in them appear forced.

The canons of *style*.

(1) The words and phrases that are used in sermons should be proper, clear, and explained so that even the more unlearned can comprehend them. Therefore, they should not be colloquial or corrupt, nor should they breathe a lofty style, but should occupy a middle ground, so that they keep the properties of the vernacular speech in view.

(2) One does best to discuss divine matters with the words and phrases drawn from the German Bible translation prepared by Luther. Indeed, all are agreed that Luther's translation observes the properties and the clarity of the vernacular language.

(3) Nor should one approve of the childish ostentation displayed by some which seeks the passing glory of skill and memory instead of promoting the salvation of the hearers. In such a display, a passage is cited for each and every word in the Bible. Sentences are thrown into confusion and the sense interrupted by such frequent citing of Bible passages, and the intellect and memory of the hearers are likewise thrown into confusion.

(4) It is especially important for the preacher to cite passages of Scripture that are appropriate for the proposed aim, not alien and foreign to it.

(5) Much favor is garnered for the sermon if, in citing Bible passages, the very words used in the German Bible translation are kept whole and unchanged.

(6) Analogies taken from Nature, allegories moderately and wisely employed, elegant exclamations used in the proper place, apostrophes directed to God, to the assembly of hearers, to a person's own soul, *prosopopoeia* used appropriately, etc., have no small effect on the minds of the hearers.

Because hearers are easily offended by the acrimony involved with *correction*, one can conveniently use that rhetorical figure which they call *anacoenosis*, of which there are two kinds: the first, in which judgment is deferred to the hearers themselves—are they not forced to admit that these or those sins lurk among them? that they are admonished to repent by this or that punishment? that it is the office of ministers to expose the sins of the people? In the second kind of *anacoenosis*, the minister of the Church, in assessing the vices of the hearers, mixes himself in with them, thereby tempering the bitterness of the rebuke. Examples of the first kind occur in Haggai 2:5; 1 Cor. 10:15, 21, 22; 1 Cor. 11:13, etc. Examples of the second kind are found in Isa. 53:3; Heb. 2:1; 1 Pet. 4:3. The bitterness of *epiplexis* can also be mitigated by a prayer to God: "Effect in our hearts, O God, that we may acknowledge this or that sin!" The same can be accomplished through *prosopopoeia*, if a Prophet or Apostle or God Himself is introduced, exposing our sins.

The canons of *memory*.

(1) The whole sermon is to be written down, word for word, and the whole thing should be committed to memory so that it may be tested, especially at the very beginning of this exercise. But this should be changed, as time progresses, since it overly debilitates the memory.

(2) Nevertheless, one should not only write down the summary headings of the outline, but really (as they say) everything, and even with Latin words, since everything can be summarized more concisely and more sharply with them.

(3) The sayings of Scripture which do not yet cling to one's memory should be written down completely with Ger-

man words, and likewise every emphasis of the expressions and phrases should be noted in the vernacular.

(4) It aids the memory greatly if some space is left between the principal parts of the sermon, so that one knows when to breathe, and so that a spatial aid may be furnished to the memory.

(5) The best aid for memory is an accurate arrangement of the text.

(6) The memory is to be exercised in one's youth by learning by heart every day those underlined Bible passages which occur in one's cursory reading. When the reading of any book is completed, each and every one of those passages can be repeated from memory.

(7) No one should place such confidence in his own memory that he neglects to have with him a set of notes when he preaches, in which the chief headings of the sermon are written down.

The canons of *delivery* and using gestures.

(1) In the delivery, one must take special care that he does not appear artificial, but that each one act in accord with his own personality.

(2) At the beginning of the sermon, the delivery should be slower; it should rise up as the sermon progresses; it should be faster at the end.

(3) One must especially and diligently flee from monotony.

(4) The delivery should be adapted to the subject matters at hand. In *instruction, training and comfort*, it should be more

sedated; in *reproof and correction*, more passionate and poignant. The same goes for exclamations, apostrophes, *prosopopoeia*, etc.

(5) Those who are just beginning to practice their sermons should work on a slow delivery, for it is easier to correct a slow delivery later than it is to correct one that is too fast.

(6) The preacher should maintain seriousness in his face and dignity in his whole body.

(7) Using gestures is appropriate, as proven—at least for the most part—among the older and experienced Theologians. But the younger ones should refrain from gesticulations and clapping.

(8) Most of all, one must beware of an excessive use of gestures. For it is one thing to be a preacher, another to be an actor.

Section 5: The fifth year of theological study.

The fifth year of theological study will be devoted to: (1) the knowledge of Church History; (2) the reading of Luther's writings; (3) of the Fathers' writings; (4) of the Scholastics' writings; all without neglecting the reading of the Bible and the treatment of controversies.

Chapter 1.

The knowledge of Church History.

The knowledge of Church History that we have put off until the final year of theological study is to be understood concerning the firmer, fuller, and more accurate knowledge of it. For it will have been worth the effort to learn a certain rudimentary and general pre-theory from Dr. Pappus' *Epitome* right away during the first year of theological study. The final year's task, then, will be to pursue the writers, both ancient and modern, of Church History, such as:

Josephus and his *De antiquitatibus Judaicis* and *De bello Judaico*.

Eusebii, Ruffini, Socratis, Theodoreti, Sozomeni, Theodori, Evagrii & Dorothei Historia sex prope seculorum res in Ecclesia gestas complectens, in one volume, published in Basle from the translation of Musculus in the year 1570*.

From the histories of Socrates, Theodoret, and Sozomenus.

Cassiodorus, chancellor of Theoderic of Verona, King of Italy, put together a volume consisting of twelve books which is commonly known as *Tripartita*.

Following them is Nicephorus, who wrote a Church History of eighteen books covering the period from the birth of Christ until the year 625, with five more books of his added later. (He lived around the year 1250.) But Nicephorus should be read with discernment, because his work contains many fables, wherefore some call him the 'Pliny of Theologians,' removing Nicephorus from the list.

Zonaras, Nicetas, Nicephorus Gregoras, Laonicus Chalcondilas, who mainly described the history of the Eastern Church. (Zonaras until the year 1117; Nicetas till 1203; Gregoras from the year 1204 up to 1341.)

The *Chronicles* of Prosperus and Marcellinus, Orosius, Sulpitius, Sigebertus Gemblacensis, and the *Chronicon Trithemii* take on the task of weaving together the History of the Eastern Church.

---

*   Hegesippus chronicled the events from the Passion of Christ until his own time, that is, A.D. 148. Eusebius, from the birth of Christ until the time of Constantine the Great, A.D. 325. Ruffinus, from the Nicene Council until the year 400. Socrates, from the end of Eusebius until the year 444. Theodoret, from the end of Eusebius until the same end. Sozomenus covers the same time span. Evagrius, from the Council of Ephesus, that is, from the year 435 until the year 595.

The collection that encompasses the summary and the principal chapters of all of these is the *Centuriae Magdeburgensis*, in thirteen volumes, by Flacius, Wigand, Mathaeus Judex, Basilius Faber, etc.

From that collection, the *Epitome* was compiled, and the *Centuries* that were still lacking were added by Lucas Osiander, of which the Sixteenth Century is especially worthy of reading, inasmuch as it abundantly and clearly explains the history of the last century.

Also to be added to the list are the *Centenarii lectionum memorabilium Johannis Wolfu*, covering in twelve volumes the mass of information that is most worth knowing. What stands out among these *Centuries* are the things they chronicle from the birth of Christ until our own time against the increasing errors and papal superstitions.

The reading of Sleidanus and Thuanus should likewise not be neglected.

If anyone felt the need to confirm our judgment about the above-named works, he could add the reading of Baronius' *Annales*, concerning which Pithaeus has rightly judged that their chief and practically only aim is to prop up papal superiority and dominion.

The *Historia Lombardica* is, itself, said to be golden, but composed by a "man of iron mouth and heart" (as Ludov. Vives says).

The lies of Surius and Chochlaeus could be considered along the way, as the shame of the Babylonian harlot is presented rather conspicuously.

Of the remaining chronicles, the ones to be preferred are of Funk, Buchholzer, and Reusner in their *Isagoges*, but especially to be commended to students are the *Tabulae Chronologicae Helvici, Itinerarium Büntingi & Theatrum terrae sanctae Adrichomii*. These are very useful for rightly understanding Biblical topography.

It is also useful to turn to the profane histories, since they can contribute something to the understanding of certain sacred histories, and especially to rightly applying the prophecies of Daniel. Therefore, the following should be read:

Berossus (fragments of whom are found in Diodorus Siculus), touching on the history of the Assyrian monarchy.

Herodotus, Thucydides, Xenophon, Diodorus Siculus, who were writers of the Persian monarchy.

Polybius, Appianus, who explain the history of the Greek Monarchy.

Livy, from whom Florus has compiled an epitome, Salustius, Caesar, Suetonius, etc., explaining the events that transpired during the Roman monarchy.

Sabellicus and Plutarchus provide a library of various histories.

We have chosen to list all these writers, not as if they could or should all be read in a single year, but so that it might be understood which authors should be read over the course of the years to come. It is sufficient in the fifth year of studies to read the *Antiquities* of Josephus and the *Church History* of Eusebius and the rest of the writers connected to him. There is no need for us to say much about the utility of knowing Church

History, since no one of reasonably sound judgment could doubt such a thing. (1) It aids in explaining sacred history. (2) It testifies to the preservation of the Church against the assaults of heretics and persecutions. (3) It provides examples of virtues and vices, of rewards and punishments, wherefore Nazianzen calls history the 'united philosophy.' (4) It enhances the mind with honest recreation, and it tempers the more serious studies, wherefore we also consider that the afternoon hours should be devoted to the study of history.

CHAPTER 2.

THE READING OF THE WRITINGS OF LUTHER.

The writings of Luther can and should also be offered in the previous years, together with other interpreters and warriors, in the accurate reading of the Bible and in the treatment of controversies. But in this fifth year of studies, one should begin to engage them in order. For Melanchthon's judgment of Luther is very true (in *praefat. partis 3. in Genesin.*): "Luther's expositions and writings are to be preferred far above all others, and for many reasons." Indeed, the Papist Malius also confessed: "On one page of Luther's writings is found more genuine and theological scholarship than in many writings of the Fathers." Wellerus (in *consil. de stud. Theolog.* edit. Anno 617.): "No one can become a distinguished theologian who truly instructs and comforts consciences, unless he has spent a long time reading Luther's writings, turning them over and over in his hand by day and by night." And afterward: "Luther translated the Prophetic and Apostolic Scriptures with more dexterity and clarity than any translator has ever been or will ever be able to do. Martin Luther alone had the skill to be able to take difficult matters and say and write them so clearly, simply, and transparently that even children can understand his writings. The same cannot be said of any other exegete."

The reading should begin in the German books from the fifth volume printed in Jena, containing the history of the Augsburg Confession, and thus one should proceed in order until the end. In the Latin writings, the reading should begin with Luther's exposition of Genesis, which was his Cygnean sermon. Other selections can also be offered for the first reading so that those writings and commentaries which are written more accurately and poignantly may be preferred to the rest, such as the second commentary on the Epistle to the Galatians, or on John 14–17, or the book on the last words of David, on Councils and the Church, etc. Only then should one return to the earlier volumes in which there is found some Papistic leaven, wherefore they should be read at a later time and with careful discretion. We shall note Luther's admonition in this matter, written in the year 1545 in the preface to the first Latin volume: "Above all, I ask the pious reader, and I ask for the sake of our Lord Jesus Christ Himself, to read these things with discretion—indeed, with a good deal of pity—and to know that I was at one time a monk and a raging Papist; that, when I undertook this endeavor, I prepared for it as a drunk, submersed as I was in the dogmas of the Pope; that, if I could have, I would have consented to kill or cooperated with those who kill anyone who disparaged obedience to the Pope with even a single syllable, etc. So it is that you will find in these earlier writings of mine how many and what great things I most humbly conceded to the Pope—things which, in later writings, and in these, I regard and abhor as the greatest blasphemy and abomination. Therefore, devout reader, you will attribute this error, or as they themselves brand it, this rebellion of mine, to the time and to my ignorance."

CHAPTER 3.

THE READING OF THE FATHERS.

PART 1.

The writings of the Fathers are not the standard of truth in the Church. Before we discuss the expected things about the utility of reading the ancient Church writers who are honored with the title 'Fathers,'* we must, first of all, advise that the writings of the Fathers must be accurately distinguished from the writings of the Prophets and Apostles, nor should they be judged to have equal authority with them. The Sacred Scripture alone, encompassing the canonical books of the Prophets and Apostles, is the only and perfect rule of truth in matters of faith, against which all the opinions and writings of all men, including the Fathers themselves, must be examined as with a Lydian stone, and to which alone one must appeal in all contro-

---

*   Augustine, commenting on Psalm 45, restricts the title 'Fathers' to the Apostles alone; he agrees that the rest of the bishops were content with the title 'sons.' Epiphanius (*contra Aerium*) distinguishes the bishops from the presbyters in this way, that the former beget Fathers of the Church through ordination, while the latter beget sons of the Church through Baptism. It can thus be said in a subordinate way of every minister, insofar as he is a servant of God, who begets us through the Word of truth (James 1:18, 1 Cor. 4:15).

versies of the faith, as to the highest and self-confirming* judge. There are two sides to this assertion. (1) *That the Scripture alone is the standard and rule of truth in matters of faith.* (2) *That the writings of the Fathers are not the standard or rule in matters of faith.* Each part of the assertion must be reinforced.

We demonstrate the part concerning the Scripture on the following grounds: (1) Scripture is *perfect*, that is, it contains everything that is necessary for faith and morals, and thus for the way of obtaining salvation (Psa. 19:7; 2 Tim. 3:16, etc.). And it is *clear* (Psa. 19:9; Psa. 119:105; 2 Pet. 1:19, etc.). Therefore, it needs neither a foreign patch nor an outside light in teaching and deciding matters of faith. (2) The Holy Spirit grants the title of 'standard' and 'judge' to Scripture alone (Psa. 20:4**; John 12:48; Heb. 4:12, etc.). (3) God everywhere calls His people back to the Word as the only rule of faith and piety (Deu. 4:2; Deu. 12:32; Is. 8:20; Luke 16:27, etc.). (4) Christ and the Apostles refute the adversaries of the truth only from the Scriptures and call their hearers only to the Scriptures (John 5:39; Mat. 22:29; Acts 18:28; Acts 26:22, etc.). (5) When the authenticity of religion and of divine worship were contaminated with heresies, with the idolatries of wickedness, etc., it was only restored through the benefit of the Word alone. The entire history of the Old and New Testaments confirms this.

The second part of the assertion receives its force from the first. For if the Holy Scripture alone is the rule of truth in matters of faith, then it is obvious that the writings of the Fathers are not the rule. This is further confirmed on the following grounds:

---

*   αὐτόπιστος
**   Vulgate Psalm 19:5

(1) The Fathers themselves remove the canonical authority, that is, equal authority with the Scriptures, from their own writings. Jerome (*Apolog. contra Jovin.*): "I do not at any time interpret the Scriptures from myself, but I speak freely from my understanding, no matter who faults me." And (in *Epist. ad Theoph.*, near the middle): "On the one hand, I have the Apostles; on the other, the rest of those who handle the Scripture. I know that the former always speak the truth, just as I know that the latter, as men, sometimes err." Cyril of Jerusalem (*Catech. 4.*): "Do not simply believe me when I present these things to you, unless you receive a demonstration from the divine Scriptures of those things which I say." Augustine (*Epist. 19. ad Hieronym. c.* Ego solid. dist. 19.): "I do not think you want your books to be read in the same way as those of the Prophets and Apostles, of whose writings it is wicked to doubt that they are free of all error." (*Epist. 48. ad Vincent.*): "[The letters and writings of the bishops] are not read in such a way that one is not allowed to dissent, if perhaps they understood something differently than the truth demands," wherefore he concludes in the same place that this kind of literature should be distinguished from the canonical writings. (*Epist. 112. ad Paulinam.*): "If something is clearly and authoritatively affirmed in the divine Scriptures, namely, those which, in the Church, are called 'canonical,' it is to be believed without any doubt. But if it is suggested that you should believe something based on other witnesses or testimonies, you are free to believe it or not to believe it for yourself. You should weigh carefully how much merit it has or does not have for establishing its credibility. For the truth is found in all sorts of places, but the authority is far from equal." He repeats the same thing in several places (lib. 2. *contra Donatist.* cap. 3.; libr. 2. *contra Crescon.* cap. 31.; *de bon. persev.* cap. 21.; *de Nat. & grat.* cap. 61.; in prol. lib. 3. *de Trinit.* cap. 3.; lib. 1. *contra Faustum* cap. 5.; cf. locum *de Eccles.* p. 1022.).

(2) The Fathers send us back to the Scripture as the only standard of faith and permit anyone the freedom to judge their own writings from it. Origen (in cap. 3. *Rom.*):"If such and so great an Apostle (Paul) does not believe that the authority of his own writings can suffice, unless he demonstrates that what he says was written in the Law and the Prophets, how much more should we, who are much less, observe this, that, when we teach, we should not present our own sentences, but those of the Holy Spirit!" Augustine (*de unitat. Eccles.* c. 3.):"Let us not hear,'This I say!' or,'This you say!' but,'This is what the Lord says!'" Basil (*Epist. 80. ad Eustathium.*): "Let us stand by the judgment of the Holy Scripture inspired by God. And let the judgment of truth be ascribed to those among whom the dogmas are found to be in harmony with the divine oracles."

(3) The standard in matters of faith should be self-confirming, but the opinions and writings of the Fathers are not self-confirming. Ambrose (libr. 1. *ad Gratianum de fide* cap. 4.):"Holy Emperor, I do not want you to believe on the basis of an argument or our interpretation. Let us ask the Scriptures! Let us ask the Apostles! Let us ask the Prophets! Let us ask Christ!" Augustine (*Epist. 19. ad Hieron.*):"Other writers—the non-canonical ones—I read in such a way that, no matter how much they excel in holiness and doctrine, I do not consider something to be true because they themselves thought it, but because they managed to persuade me, either through those canonical authors or by plausible reason, that they do not differ from the truth." Origen (homil. 1. in *Jerem.*):"It is necessary for us to call on the Holy Scriptures to testify, for clearly our opinions and expositions are unreliable apart from these witnesses."

(4) The standard should be constant and immutable. But the writings of the Fathers did not always exist in the

Church. Therefore, they are not the standard. For if the writings of the Fathers were the standard of truth, what was the standard in the Church when no writings of the Fathers yet existed? Just as the Word was, at that time, the only standard of truth, so it still remains today. God revealed His Word to this end and chose to have it reduced to letters, that there might be a constant rule of truth in the Church. But the Fathers surely did not write to this end, that their writings might become the Church's authentic standard of truth, nor to rob the Church of its freedom, but chiefly that they might serve the people of their day and make known the controversies that were being promoted and stirred up at that time.

(5) The standard of truth in matters of faith should be free and devoid of all error. But the writings of the Fathers are not devoid of all error. This could be demonstrated with many examples. The stalks of erroneous opinions certainly also appear in the most ancient Fathers of the pious ages: on the millennial kingdom of Christ, on the salvation of the Gentiles, on the illicit affairs of angels, on monogamy, on the powers of free will, on the impassibility of the flesh of Christ, etc.

(6) The standard of truth is unbending and always in agreement with itself. But the Fathers, in their writings, are not in constant agreement either with themselves or with others. Bellarmine (lib. 5. *de Pontif. Rom.* cap. 6.): "I refer to Jerome. In his commentary on Malachi, he did not think that Malachi was talking about the actual Elijah, but in his commentary on Matthew 11 and 17, he thought and taught the opposite." One can gather just from the disputations of Bellarmine how diverse—yes, how contrary to one another—their expositions of Scripture are. Convinced by this light of truth, even the Papists themselves deny from time to time that the writings of

the Fathers are the standard of truth in matters of faith. Biel (lect. 41. in *canon. Miss.*): "The authority of the holy Fathers does not compel anyone to assent to their sayings, unless they are founded on the divine Scriptures or rely on divine revelation." Cajetan (in *praefat. com. in Genes.*) admits that he has occasionally departed from the torrent of the doctors and adds: "For God did not bind the exposition of Scripture to the opinions of the doctors, or else all hope of explaining the Scriptures would be removed from us, except by transferring a book onto five sheets." Roffensis (in *confut. Luth. prooem. par. Et nos.*): "Even we do not deny that the Fathers occasionally erred." Alphonsus de Castro (lib. 1. *adv. haeres. c.* 7.) refutes the interpretation of dist. 9. that the writings of the Fathers are commanded to be kept today down to the last *iota.* "Where are they commanded? Or how can they be prescribed today, when the opinions of the holy Fathers often disagree with one another? Surely God cannot prescribe contradictory things!" Canus (lib. 7. *locor. Theol.* cap. 3. num. 7.): "The canonical authors, as superior, celestial, and divine, preserve a perpetual and steadfast constancy. But the rest of the holy writers are inferior and human; they fail now and then and sometimes give birth to a monster, going astray from the proper order and institution of Nature." Baronius (tom. 1. *annal. an.* 34. par. 213.): "In the interpretation of the Scriptures, the Catholic Church does not always or in all things follow the most holy Fathers, whom we call Doctors of the Church on account of their sublime erudition, no matter how much it may be established that they were imbued before others with the grace of the Holy Spirit." Salmeron (in *epist. ad Rom.* Disputat. 6., shortly before the end): "In reading the Fathers, it seems best to observe the judgment of Quintilianus, who writes thus: 'Neither should the reader be at once convinced that all the things said by the great authors are always perfect, for they occasionally slip and yield to the burden. They indulge the pleasure of their talents. They are the greatest men, but they are still men. And it occurs to the readers that whatever they discover among them is a rule of language, so that the lower things are imitated, etc." Bellarmine (lib. 3. *de verbo Dei* cap. 10. par. dices): "Who denies that the Fathers had the gift of interpretation, or that even the best of them slipped and fell?" Bellarmine again (lib. cap. 3. par. de ipso): "Because the literal sense was abandoned, several of them fell at times into the gravest of errors. Take Origen, for example, who erred because he took figuratively things which were to be taken simply. Others, like Papias, Justin, Tertullian, Lactantius, etc., fell for the opposite reason; they took simply and properly things which were to be taken figuratively." (lib. 2. *de council.* cap. 12.): "The writings of the Fathers are not authoritative, nor do they have binding authority." (lib. 1. *de sanct. beatit.* cap. 6.): "I do not see how to defend Justin, Irenaeus, Epiphanius, and Oecumenius, who thought that the demons are not punished with the penalty of hell before the Last Day." (lib. 2. *de sanct. beatit.* cap. 4.): "Lactantius fell into many errors, especially concerning the coming age, since he was more of an expert in the books of Cicero than he was in the Holy Scriptures. Erudition was lacking to Victorinus, although the desire for erudition was not lacking." (lib. 2. *de purgat.* cap. 6.): "Procopius, Eucherius, and Isidorus are uncertain and obscure authors." In chapter 8, he assigns Origen to eternal fire. Villavincentius (*de rad. stud. Theolog.* lib. 4. cap. 6): "It is clear that all the Fathers, for as much as they were outstanding in erudition and innocence of life, repeatedly offend with their word and writings." The Dominican Sixtus Senensis not only acknowledges that the Fathers erred very often, but he also zealously gathered their errors in explaining the Scripture together and filled two whole books with them which he added to his holy library, saying that "it could not be concealed that their errors were not without offense to Catholic piety, nor without great disturbance to the readers." More things in this matter, namely, concerning the errors of the Fathers, are found in Erasmus (in *annot. super cap. 2. Matth.* p. 13; *super cap.* 11. *Matth.* p. 41; *super cap.* 17. *Matth.* p. 58.; *super cap.* 22. *Luc.* cap. 157.) and in Ludo. Vives (in lib. 12. *de civ. Dei* cap. 15.; lib. 16. cap. 34; lib. 18. cap. 44.). See also Luther (in *enarrat. cap. 1. Genes.* p. 13.; in cap. 2. p. 27.; in cap. 3. pag. 53.; *lib. de abrog. Miss. priv.*; in *libr. contra Regem Angliae*, etc.).

Part 2.

The writings of the Fathers are not to be eliminated from the Church. Indeed, they are justly used against the Papists, who are constantly insisting on the authority of the Fathers and extolling them too highly. Nonetheless, their writings should by no means simply be eliminated from the Church, nor should they be removed from the hands of the Candidates of Theology, but they are altogether to be retained because of the benefits to be expected, not despised, from reading them. Some authority is owed to the writings of the Fathers, even if divine authority is denied them. They are not the judges of faith, but witnesses and bearers of it. They are not gods, but brilliant lights. Therefore, so that a better judgment may be made, we proceed.

Some of the writings of the Fathers are *exegetical*, in which the books of Scripture are explained. Some are *elenctic*, in which the errors of heretics are overturned. Some are *dogmatic*, in which the people in the assembly of the Church are instructed, to which may also be added the *paraenetic*, *paramythetic*, and *nouthetic* writings, in which they exhort, comfort, reprove, etc. From all these a certain benefit can be gained.

(1) The *exegetical* writings serve us in the interpretation of Scripture. They *serve* us, I say; they do not serve as our masters. For by no means do we assert with the Papists that "the interpretation of Scripture is bound to the authority of the Church, that is, of the Fathers." By no means do we approve of such a rule of interpretation in which, when someone proceeds to explain some saying, he especially and first of all searches for the interpretations of the Fathers. Such a method is revealed in Bellarmine's disputations. But when we affirm that the writings of the Fathers serve us in the interpretation of Sacred Scripture, we want it to be understood in this way: First of all, the true and genuine sense of any passage is to be sought from the aim, from the things that come before and after, from the original languages, from the analogy of faith, etc. Only then can the pertinent interpretations of the Fathers be added, that it may be shown that our interpretation is not new, but was already present in the early Church, close to the time of the Apostles. For sometimes the Fathers show us in their writings some hidden sense in the Scriptures which we, perhaps, with our own ingenuity, could not have elicited from them. To this, Philipp Melanchthon applies the dictum of Samson in Judges 14:18: "If you had not plowed with my heifer, you would not have discovered my riddle." If God wanted to admonish Moses, the wisest of men, about a very serious matter through Jethro the Midianite, how much more shouldn't we conclude that we can be taught many things by the writings of such excellent men!

The interpretations of the Fathers are, of course, not to be considered authoritative nor placed on an equal level with the canonical Scriptures. But with a grateful and pious mind we should acknowledge and praise their efforts, because they were special instruments of the Holy Spirit and because they provided service to the Church which was being gathered to Christ at that time. 1 The. 5:19–21: "Do not extinguish the Spirit. Do not despise prophecies. Test all things. Hold onto what is good."

If we do not entirely reject the commentaries of the more modern doctors of the Church, but with a grateful mind make use of their efforts in explaining Scripture, then we should most certainly not entirely reject the exegetical writings of the Fathers. It is certainly true that most of them were ignorant of the Hebrew language*, wherefore they sometimes fail miserably in the interpretation of Scripture and depart from the proper and genuine sense of a passage. But in very many passages they head straight to the truth, following a straight path. Therefore, God did not choose in vain to preserve the writings of the purer antiquity, but wanted them to serve as a tool for investigating the meaning of Scripture, so that the minds of the pious might be more steadfastly confirmed from the fact that the true meaning of Scripture was already well-known.

(2) The *elenctic* writings, by which heresies are opposed, to which also pertain the *didactic* writings, in which they explain and confirm the articles of faith, show us the perpetual consensus of the Catholic Church in the fundamental articles. Naturally, we do not state with the Papists that the writings of the Fathers are the standard of truth in the articles of faith, but the consensus of antiquity concerning the truth is not to be despised, for what could be more gratifying to the pious mind than to view the consanguinity of doctrine (as Tertullian calls it**) which our churches have with the early Church? The Pa-

---

*   *linguae sanctae*
**   *lib. de praescript.*

pists continually incriminate our doctrine with the accusation of novelty and offend the eyes of many in this way, wherefore we rightly appeal to that "Ancient of Days" (Dan. 7:13), from whom our doctrine went out in the most ancient tablets of divine truth, namely, in the Prophetic and Apostolic writings. But it is well worth the effort, in tempering the accusations of the adversaries more forcefully, to seek support for our opinion from the writings of the ancients, especially of those who were closest to the time of the Apostles, which the perpetual practice of the Church shows to be right.

Augustine (lib. 4. *contra duas Epist. Pelagian.* cap. 8.): "Since the Church of Christ, both Western and Eastern, shuddered at the profane novelties of the Pelagians' expressions, I think it pertains to our care, not only to summon the canonical Holy Scriptures against those witnesses, which we have already sufficiently done, but also to offer other documents from the writings of the saints who handled the Scriptures before us with celebrated fame and with immense glory. Not that we consider the authority of any debater to be equal to that of the canonical books, as if there was nothing that was perceived to be better or truer by one Catholic than by another who is likewise a Catholic; but that they may be admonished who think that these men are saying something in the same way that the Catholic teachers followed the divine utterances about these matters prior to the new and idle utterances of these men; and that they may know that the genuine and anciently founded Catholic faith is being defended by us against the recent presumption and mischief of the Pelagian heretics."

Basil (in *serm. contra Sabell. & Arium*) thunders against the novel discoveries of the heretics. "May tradition restrain you! The Lord taught in this way, the Apostles preached it,

208

the Fathers preserved it, the Martyrs confirmed it. You should be content to speak as you have been taught." And afterwards: "We encourage you to do, not what you please, but what pleases the Lord, and is in harmony with the Scriptures, and is not contrary to the Fathers."

Therefore, when the testimonies of the Fathers agree with the oracles of Scripture, then those admonitions are in order from Deu. 32:7: "Remember the days of old. Ask your father, and he will declare it to you; your old men, and they will tell you." From Pro. 22:8: "Do not move the ancient boundary which your ancestors put in place." From Ecclesiasticus 8:11*: "Do not stray from the story of the elderly, for they themselves learned from their parents, and you will learn understanding from them." From Jeremiah 6:16: "Thus the LORD has said, 'Stand on the roads, and see, and ask about the ancient paths, what the good road is, and walk on it. So you will find rest for your soul.'"

But when the ancients stray from the path of Scripture, then the words of Ezekiel 20:18–19 apply: "Do not walk in the statutes of your fathers. I am the LORD your God. Walk in My precepts." Mat. 23:9–10: "Do not call anyone on earth your father, for you have one Father, who is in heaven. Nor shall you call anyone 'Teacher,' for you have one Teacher, the Christ." 1 Cor. 7:23: "You were bought at a price. Do not become slaves of men."

The Papists are constantly promoting the testimonies of the Fathers. But we give them the same reply that Athanasius already gave long ago (tom. 2. *de sent. Dionysii Arianis*): "Seeing that they can find nothing in the Scripture to support their

---

*   vid. Vulgate

heresy, they turn to the Fathers like robbers, since they listen poorly with respect to their own studies. They pretend that the Fathers are their good and honest associates, and they flee to them just as the Jews fled to Father Abraham when they were convicted by the Scripture." The *Expurgatorii Indices*[*] testify, but especially Junius (in *praefat. Indicis expurgatorii*, which he himself published), how the writings of the Fathers are treated by the Papists: "They shave, blot out, add, alter, subtract, substitute." As Erasmus says (in *praefat. Hilarii*): "Whatever they leave intact and inviolate in them, they twist into a foreign sense." The theologians of the University of Douai do not deny this, for they write in the censure of Bertram, whom they introduced in the *Expurgatorius Index*, saying that, "When they function as Opponents in disputations, they bring in many errors from other Catholic Fathers against Bertram. They minimize them, excuse them, very often deny them with a contrived explanation, and attach an agreeable sense to them." But who could have made a correct judgment from those corruptions and distortions, if he was clearly only a visitor in the reading of the Fathers?

All prudent and piously learned men acknowledge that Master Chemnitz, that incomparable theologian, provided a most useful work in his *Examination of the Council of Trent*, in which he did not choose to refute the papistic errors from the Scripture alone, but also from the testimonies of the Fathers. Chemnitz stands in the footprints of Luther in the Leipzig Colloquy. Practically all orthodox theologians stand in the footprints of Luther and Chemnitz as they add the support of the Fathers to the testimonies of Scripture.

---

[*]   There are three *Expurgatorii Indices*: the Belgian, the Roman, and the Spanish.

Furthermore, I would certainly not hesitate to suggest that the pious and Christian mind is in no small way confirmed in knowledge of the truth and is fortified against the papistic clamor about the antiquity of the Roman Catholic doctrine, if he understands from the writings of the Fathers with what steps the Roman Bishop ascended to that lofty peak of Antichristian tyranny; what the occasion was for the seeds of papal errors, first lightly sown in that broadest of fields, to grow; in what stages they departed from the simplicity and sincerity of Apostolic doctrine. I would note that in the coronis of Dr. Hunnius' work (in *quaest. & respons. de praedest.* tom. 1. operum col. 901.) there is a beautiful passage about the search for this consensus of antiquity in the articles of faith: "I do not deny that the Fathers or ecclesiastical writers wrote in various ways about various articles. But the truth remains that, in confirming all the articles of the Christian religion, certain clear sayings and testimonies can be offered from their writings. So if the [Huberian] dogma [of universal election] were revealed in Holy Scripture, how is it possible that, throughout the course of so many centuries, even for the entire existence of the Christian Church, nothing should have been passed down concerning it?" And afterwards: "We know that the Fathers or ecclesiastical writers had their moles and errors in different articles. But this remains fixed and firm, that it is impossible to demonstrate any topic in the whole of theology whose express testimonies are not found in that learned antiquity, if not with this Father, then certainly with another, if not with all, yet with some. Nor will it be possible to find a single instance that proves this assertion incorrect or that even weakens it."

(3) The *demegoric* writings of the Fathers and the things that belong to them—the nouthetic, paramythetic, paraenetic,

etc.—provide useful opinions which instill a zeal for piety. We do not deny that the perfect rule for shaping one's life and morals is properly set forth for us in the Scriptures. But those pithy and poignant sentences of the ancients have no small effect on piously educated men as they express, with different words, the very thing which is taught in the Scriptures. I think it is outside of the realm of controversy that there existed in the Church greater piety, conscience, and zeal in those early days, close to the age of the Apostles, than in the worn-out and cold old age of these last days of men.

PART 3.

How the writings of the ancients are to be read. If the reading of the Fathers is to be fruitful, the following rules will have to be observed:

(1) Since (as we have just demonstrated) the writings of the Fathers, are neither the rule of truth, nor entirely free from error, nor are they to be made equal with the canonical books of Scripture, discretion must be employed in reading them, just as all things must be examined according to the standard of Scripture, and only those things which are right, salutary, and useful should be chosen, after rejecting the opinions that are harmful and troublesome. 1 The. 5:21: "Test all things. Hold onto what is good." Lactantius (lib. 2. de orig. err. cap. 8.) says that "they deprive themselves of wisdom who approve the discoveries of their ancestors without any judgment and are led by them in the manner of sheep." Basil (in *moralib.* reg. 4.): "It behooves the hearer to test everything that is said by the doctors, to receive the things that are in harmony with the Scriptures and to reject those that are foreign." Jerome (in *Epist. ad Miner.*): "My judgment is to read the ancients, to test

everything, to retain the things that are good and that do not deviate from the faith of the Church." He shows the same thing (praefat. in *Oseam*), with what liberty he read the expositions of others on the same Prophet—think Apollinarius, Origen, Pierius, Eusebius, Didymus, etc.: "I say these things that you may know whom I have as forerunners in this field of the Prophets, whom also, I admit to your discretion, out of simplicity and not out of pride (as one of my friends hisses), I have not followed in all things, so that I appear to be a judge of their work rather than an interpreter." Erasmus (in *praefat. Hilar.*): "God wanted this peculiar good fortune to belong only to the divine volumes: that there is no error in them. Otherwise, there is no one so learned and insightful that he does not slip, that he is not sometimes blind, etc." Luther (in *cap.* 3. *Genes.* p. 53.): "It is necessary, especially for novices in Holy Scripture, that when they go to read the ancient doctors, they read them with discretion, or rather, with a definite plan to condemn the things that are less than commendable, lest they be deceived by the authority of the name 'Fathers and Doctors of the Church.'"

(2) To the reading of the Fathers should be introduced the idea of genuine theology, conceived from the Sacred Scriptures and firmly fixed in the mind, so that by them, as by the guidance of the shining Little Dipper, one can learn to navigate around those many boulders that often threaten those who sail the vast ocean. This is also why we postponed the reading of the Fathers until the fifth year of theological study.

(3) The genuine and authentic writings of the Fathers must be carefully discerned from the adulterated and counterfeit writings. For many writings are introduced onto the stage of the Church today under the venerable disguise of the Fathers. They have been composed, or certainly corrupted, by

heretics. The author of the exposition of the Creed among the works of Cyprian, who is believed to have been Rufinus, warns: "They were perverse men who, to defend their dogmas, introduced certain things under the name of holy men which those holy men never wrote." Gelasius (in *c. Sancta Romana* dist. 5.) lists a truly copious hodgepodge of books which the heretics wanted to impose on the early Church under the name of the Apostles. Do we really think that the same was not frequently done with the writings of the Fathers?

Eusebius (lib. 3. *Histor. Eccles.* capit. 38.) testifies that many things appeared long ago that were fabricated and concocted under the name of Clement. The Macedonians took care to circulate a certain book with many copies under the name of Cyprian; and they made it available for a meager penny, so that buyers, enticed both by the martyr's title and by the cheap price, might procure it more easily and read it more avidly. The Eutychians published the writings of Apollinarius under the name of Athanasius. The African Fathers—Augustine among them—uncovered a Roman deception at the Council of Carthage in adulterating the canons of the Nicene Creed. Nicephorus (lib. 15. *Hist.* cap. 16.) reports that certain documents of Cyril were corrupted by Timothy Aelurus. Many bewailed long ago that the same thing had happened to certain works of Origen, as Jerome reports (*ad Pammachium*). Even Sixtus Senensis acknowledges that those corruptions have been introduced in the old writings (praefat. lib. 5. *Bibliothec.*), saying: "The complaint of Pamphylus Martyr, Eusebius Caesariensis, Didymus, and Rufinus should not be ignored, namely, that many of the writings of Clement, Dionysius, Origen, Athanasius, and other noble doctors were long ago treated terribly by the heretics, who won confidence and authority for their heresies under the name of the most excellent Fathers. They also grafted many irreconcilable parts of their own dogmas onto the things which those famous men thought and taught. It is not credible that the Fathers either thought or taught contradictory things in the same volumes, on the same subject, and at the same time, especially since they were neither insane nor entirely oblivious." Ludov. Vives (in lib. 22. *de civ. Dei* cap. 8.): "There is no doubt that many things were added by those who used to contaminate all the writings of great men with their unclean hands."

Many centuries ago the writings of the Fathers lay hidden in the libraries of the monks, who often copied them down with errors, since typography had not yet been invented. Kimedoncius (lib. 2. *de Script. autoritate* cap. 6.): "I call as witnesses the libraries of so many monasteries throughout the papal realm, in some of which I myself saw the monks brazenly apply their deceitful hands to the ecclesiastical writers, erasing whole sentences and entire pages—indeed, shamefully castrating the authors by cutting out whole sections and books. Sometimes they even changed at will the things which seemed difficult to them."

It cannot be explained briefly or sufficiently lamented with how much rashness, or shall I say audacity, these things are still today being falsified by the Jesuits. (See Junius' *praef. in Indic. Expurgat.*) Nor should that which Sixtus Senensis writes be denied (in *Epist. dedicate. Bibliothecae praefixa ad Pium V.*): "[The Papists] were careful to cleanse and correct all the writings of the Catholic authors, and especially the writings of the ancient Fathers that had been infected with the poison and contaminated with the dregs of the heretics of this age." The Papist Michael Thomasius in a letter to Cardinal Antonius Perrenotus, prefaced with the works of Lactantius, claimed that he had freed the books of Lactantius from many errors which had been added to them by the deceit and fraud of heretics.

Sixtus (lib. 4. *Bibl.* at the end) and Billius (in *annotate. ad metaphrasin Ecclesiastae Nazianzeno asscriptam*) enumerate (from Erasmus, Rhenanus and others) various causes of false inscriptions, which can be reduced to these three main headings: that some are *honest and justifiable*, others are *excusable and pardonable*, while still others are *shameful and damnable*.

To the first class belongs the situation in which some books were written by the Fathers under a foreign name. Thus Vigilius (lib. 5. *contra Eutychein*) admits that he "had written books against Sabellius, Photinus and Arius under the name of Athanasius, as if he [that is, Athanasius] were dealing with those present, so that he might place the conversations of the Fathers with heretical men before the eyes of his age, as it were." Salvianus inscribed his books to the Catholic Church with the name 'Bishop Timothy,' explaining the reasoning of his plan (in *praefatione ad Salonium Episcopum*): "In every volume that has gone out, the name of the reading is sought more than the name of the author." Afterwards, he lists the specific reasons: "The first reason comes from the command of God in which we are ordered to avoid the vanity of earthly glory in every way, lest, in seeking the gentle breeze of human praise, we lose our heavenly reward. Second, lest the smallness of his person remove the authority from his salubrious sayings, for every saying is thought to be only as great as he who said it, etc." Vincentius Lyrinensis put out a book entitled *Peregrinus* against the profane novelty of expressions, that it might be willingly read by heretics.

To the second class belongs the situation in which some, out of ignorance and imprudence, ascribe the unattributed and anonymous writings to more ancient authors, being deceived either by a similarity of argument and style, or by the use of old letters, wrongly thought to be obsolete, or by other suspicious arguments.

To the third class belongs the situation in which books, written by others in previous centuries, are published with malicious deceit in order to support and propagate errors under the name of the ancients. Erasmus laments (praefat. *in Hieron.*): "There was a certain man whose particular zeal was, in the way of a cuckoo, to insert his own jingles into the works of others, especially of Ambrose, Augustine and Jerome, a man who is said to have had a monstrous—or rather insane—desire to pollute all the painstaking works of Jerome in every way possible, even to the point that he was not content to attach only his own letters, but also his own books to Jerome's books, like someone who sews filthy rags onto a purple emblem." Thus the names of Dionysius the Areopagite, Abdias the Babylonian, Clement the disciple of the Apostles, Anacletus and of other ancient bishops are falsely attached to books and epistles that are today read under their names*. Therefore, the prudent reader will beware, lest he allow his eyes to be weakened by the magnificent title of some writings so that he accepts dross for gold, clay for precious stones, poison for the remedy.

But by what signs and criteria the genuine are to be discerned from the counterfeits is harder to determine. They can be reduced to three main headings, namely, *time, dogmas,*

---

* The ancient authors who are not cited by their posterity and who do not have the testimony of any approved author are either undoubtedly spurious or less reliable. The books edited by the Roman librarians and which are only found in the Vatican or in the monks' cloisters are deservedly considered suspect.

and style. One must ask if the time is consistent, if the dogmas are in agreement, and if the style bears authority. Thus it
is clear that the *Quaestiones et responsiones* attributed to Justin
are not Justin's, because Origen is cited in questions 82 and
86, although Origen lived long after Justin. And in question
127, the Manichaeans are mentioned, although they were unknown until the third century after the birth of Christ. Augustine (Epist. 48.) admits that he had recognized certain writings
of Cyprian from the peculiar beauty of style. The *Epistolam ad
Felicem Papam*, which is attributed to Athanasius, cannot be
his, because it contains the phrase, "The Roman Church is the
sacred whirlpool in which all things whirl.*" But this play on
words does not and cannot exist in Greek. Therefore, it was
written instead in Latin. In the same work, it says that "it was
decreed in the Council of Nicaea that appeal should be made
to the Roman Bishop in all cases," but this assertion is not at
all appropriate for Athanasius. In *Clementis Romani ad Jacobum
Apostolum Epistolis*, there is an anachronism of more than 30
years. There were tracts published under the name of Cyril of
Alexandria in which the dogmas of souls having been created
before the world, of the penalties of the damned having an end,
etc., are promoted. But these deliria of Origen were energeti-
cally refuted elsewhere by Cyril. Many rules for recognizing
these signs can be seen in Sixtus Senensis, Erasmus, *Hyperium
de ratione Studii Theologici*, Chemnitz' *De lect. Patrum*, Perkins' *In
ementito Romanae fidei Catholicismo*, Rivetus' *in critico sacro.*

(4) In the genuine writings of the Fathers, one must
distinguish the philosophical from the theological. For since
many of them were first instructed in the disciplines of the heathen before they were converted to the Christian faith, it hap-

---

*   *Romanam Ecclesiam esse sacrum verticem, in quo omnia vertantur.*

pened that certain philosophical matters were mixed in with their writings, which can safely be left out. Thus in the first tome of the works of Augustine, in the eighth stroma of Clement of Alexandria, and in other works of the ancients, there are many purely philosophical sayings, such as certain Platonic and Aristotelian dogmas of self-determination[*], the knowledge of the Logos ingrained in all things, purgatory, perfection, etc. They likewise transferred certain rites of the heathen into the Church, so that, in this way, they might attract the Gentiles all the more to the fellowship of the Christian faith.

(5) While it is true that certain erroneous opinions are also found in the most revered Fathers of the Church—such as Justin, Irenaeus, Tertullian, Cyprian, Clement of Alexandria, Origen, Arnobius, Lactantius, Hilary, etc.—who lived close to the time of the Apostles, so that one must pay more attention to who comes closest to the writings of the Apostles than to the times of the Apostles[**], nevertheless, the more ancient are surely to be preferred to the more recent, for the closer they were to the time of the Apostles, the more genuinely they handle the divine writings and the more purely they explain the heavenly doctrine, just as a river gathers more mud and debris the farther away it is from the source.

But opinions vary as to how widely the age of the Fathers should be extended. Some think the age of the Fathers ended at the time of Augustine (Keckermann. lib. 3. *Syst. Logic.* cap. 8.), since many traditions then began to inundate the Church, which he himself laments (Ep. 119). But others extend it to the time of Gregory (*Ivell. contra Hardingum, Mylius contra Austriacum quon-*

---

[*]   αὐτεξουσία

[**]   As Christ. Agr. says (in *propugn. Antipist.*), "We believe the Church, not because she is old, but because she is sound."

dam Pontificium), for then the Antichristian domination of the Roman Pope was confirmed by Phocas, and corruptions came rushing in like a flood. Some push the age of the Fathers forward to the thousandth year after the birth of Christ, at which exact time Scholastic Theology began to reign in the Church.

If the age of the Fathers were to be defined by the overall authenticity of doctrine, it would have to be terminated shortly after the time of the Apostles, for, as Hegesippus says, according to Eusebius (lib. 3. *Eccles. Hist.* cap. 28.): "Up until the time of Trajan, about the year 110, the Church remained a pure and uncorrupted virgin, while those who tried to corrupt the sound rule of salutary preaching, if they existed then, lay hidden in a sort of obscure mist until that time. But after the holy company of Apostles came to a blessed end and that generation, which had gained the divine wisdom to hear with their ears, passed away, then a conspiracy of ungodly error began through the seduction of those who were teaching a foreign doctrine, who also, now with a bare head because none of the Apostles remained any longer, attempted to preach against the preaching of the truth, to preach from the adversary the knowledge of a false name." Eusebius practically confirms this with his own words (lib. ejusd. cap. 34.). Jerome also says (in *vita Malchi*): "When he was about to write the history from the advent of the Savior until his own times, he had decided to write from the Apostles up until the dregs of his own time, how and through whom the Church of Christ was born, how she grew up through persecutions, was crowned with the Martyrs, and, after she came to have Christian rulers, how she became greater in power and in riches, but lesser in virtues."

Therefore, since the times closest to the Apostolic Church were purer than those that followed, and since the seeds of opinions were secretly sown earlier, before they grew up into a wide field of errors, those ecclesiastical doctors whom we call Fathers for the sake of distinguishing them from the Scholastics, can be divided into three classes or orders.

To the first order pertain those who flourished from the time of the Apostles up until the Council of Nicaea, that is, until the year 325. To the second order, those who were famous from the time of the Council of Nicaea until the second Council of Constantinople, that is, until the year 681. To the third order, those who flourished from the time of the Council of Constantinople up until the beginning of Scholastic Theology, that is, until the year 1172, when Lombard, the Master of Sentences, lived.

The Fathers can also be divided into centuries or ages. Flourishing in the first century were *Ignatius, Dionysius the Areopagite, Clement of Rome.*

In the second century, *Justin, Irenaeus, Clement of Alexandria, Theophilus.*

In the third century, *Tertullian, Julius Africanus, Cyprian, Origen, Methodius, Minutius Felix.*

In the fourth century, *Eusebius Caesariensis, Lactantius, Athanasius, Arnobius, Cyril of Jerusalem, Macarius, Hilary, Gaudentius, Basil, Gregory Nazianzen, Gregory of Nyssa, Ambrose, Rufinus, Jerome, Epiphanius, Philastrius, Chrysostom.*

In the fifth century, *Optatus Milevitanus, Ephrem, Evagrius, Augustine, Prudentius, Gennadius, Hesichius, Maximus Taurinensis, Orosius, Cassianus, Cyril of Alexandria, Vincentius Lyrinensis, Synensius, Claudius Marius Victor, Eucherius, Isidorus Pelusiota, Leo*

I, *Primasius, Theodoret, Prosper, Theodulus, Sedulius, Vigilius, Gelasius, Salvianus, Fulgentius, Junilius, Salonius, Paulinus.*

In the sixth century, *Boetius, Maxentius, Eusebius, Emissenus, Cassiodorus, Aretas, Gregory of Tours, Alcimus, Fortunatus, Olimpiodorus, Gregory the Great, Isidorus Hispalensis.*

In the seventh century, *Anastasius, Sophronius, Caesarius, Andodemus.*

In the eighth century, *Bede the Presbyter, Alcuinus, Damascene, Carolus M. Paulus Diaconus.*

In the ninth century, *Haymo, Photius, Bertramus, Rahanus, Strabus Fuldensis* (the author of the ordinary gloss), *Paschasius, Remigius, Angelomus, Hincmarus, Udalricus Augustanus.*

In the tenth century, *Oecumenius, Fulbertus Carnotensis, Theophylact, Humbertus, Algerus, Euthymius, Guitmundus, Hildebertus, Giselbertus, Luitprandus, Ansbertus, Radulphys, Smaragdos.*

In the eleventh century, *Rupertus, Tuiciensis, Anselm, Florentinus, Wigorniensis, Lanfrancus, Petrus Damianus, Berno.*

In the twelfth century: *Bernard, Honorius, Augustodunensis, Nilus Archiepiscopus Thessalonicensis, Hugo de S. Victore, Theodorus Balsamon Patriarcha Antiochenus, etc.*

From all these, several writings of the Fathers exist together in *Bibliotheca Patrum, in Orthodoxographis, in Haereseologia autorum 18.*

(6) The opinions of scholars vary with regard to the order that should be observed in reading such a vast number of volumes of the Fathers. Some think a chronological order should be observed, so that those who wrote first should also

be read first. In this way it can be clearly seen how the inclination of doctrine gradually developed.

It has been the procedure of others to have Cyprian take the lead, followed by Basil and Nazianzen, and from them a transition is made to the commentaries of Jerome, Augustine, and several others.

Some judge that the writings of Ambrose are to be preferred to all the rest. Erasmus writes (in *prooem. comm. Ambr.*): "Among the Latin Doctors, I think hardly any is worthier than Dr. Ambrose, whole works of whom are extant. I would like for this to be seen—and I say it sincerely and without insulting anyone. It is not without cause that they call him the 'Honey-sweet Doctor,' whether because he is more expert in languages and the Scriptures than Jerome, more elaborate in his phrases than Hilary, keener at explaining knotty questions than Augustine. Some, likewise, may have surpassed others in gifts. But whom will you show me who handles the Sacred Letters with as much sincerity, who has avoided suspicious dogmas more cautiously, who bears the title of Christian Bishop anywhere in such a way, who breathes paternal compassion in such a way, who has combined the supreme authority of a prelate with supreme gentleness?"

Augustine is to be preferred to all the rest, and therefore it seems best that he should be read before them all. Remigius Antisiodorensis says of him: "As the sun exceeds all the planets in brilliance, he has exceeded all others in the exposition of the Scriptures." Erasmus (in *praefat. oper. August.*) makes the following comparison: "In Athanasius, we regard the sacred and sedulous clarity of teaching. In Basil, we admire, besides subtlety, a pious and sweet expressiveness. In Chrysostom, we willingly embrace a fluent richness of speech. In Cyprian, we honor a spirit worthy of martyrdom. In Hilary, we admire a grand eloquence equal to the grand material, and a lofty-style-actor, so to speak. In Ambrose, we cherish those sweet thorns and the modesty worthy of a bishop. In Jerome, we rightly praise the rich fare of the Scriptures. In Gregory, we acknowledge a pure and uncolored sanctimony. In Augustine are found all these things."

This is also Luther's judgment (tom. 3. *Jenensi Germ.* f. 368. in aliis edit. fol. 409., in libro, *quod verba Christi, Hoc est corpus meum; adhuc firmiter stent*): "After the Apostles, the Christian Church does not have, in my judgment, a more outstanding teacher than Augustine." Wellerus (in *orat. de studio Theol. Rostoch.* Ann. 617. edit.): "When I applied my mind to Theology, Luther would urge me to read certain important books of Augustine, namely, *De confessionibus, De doctrina Christiana, De civitate Dei,* and similar things. He also told me to dedicate some time now and then to reading the writings of Bernard for the distinguished sentences with which he abounds. He also wanted me to read Ambrose for a knowledge of antiquity. He discouraged me from reading Origen and similar authors, because they all transformed the passages of Scripture into allegories. Therefore, he considered the reading of Origen and similar authors to be dangerous for students of theology. Nor did he ever approve either of the style or of the interpretation of Jerome, for his style is puffed up, and he expended more effort in making speeches than in interpreting the Scripture. Nor did he praise very highly the writings of Basil, for, he said, they smack of monasticism. He did, nonetheless, want the 'Master of Sentences' to be read—with discretion—because he has compiled the sentences of nearly all the Fathers on the important topics of Christian doctrine."

Chemnitz (in *orat. de lect. Patr.*): "By the consensus of all learned men, Augustine wins the prize. He has more doctrinal content than any of the rest, and that content is also more properly and more helpfully explained than what the rest have provided."

Others prescribe yet another order for reading the writings of the Fathers. It seems most helpful in the fifth year of theological study to read the *Epistolas* of Ignatius; Justin's *Apologias* and *Dialogum cum Tryphone*; Irenaeus' *Adversus haereses*; Tertullian's *Apologeticum, De praeseriptionibus, De resurrectione carnis adversus Marcionem*; Cyprian's *Epistolas*; Nazianzen's *Orationes*; Cyril's *Catecheses*; *Didactica et Elenctica* in the third, fourth, fifth, sixth, and seventh tomes of Augustine; Damascene's *De orthodoxa fide*, etc. Afterwards, if he wishes and has time, he should observe a chronological order with the rest, except for Bernard, who alone is to be preferred to the rest after Augustine, just as Augustine is to be preferred only after the Apostles.

(7) The exegetical things that come to mind in the reading of the Fathers should be noted in those books which were mentioned above in the chapter on *the accurate reading of Scripture*. The things that pertain to confirming the controversial articles of faith should be reported in the books of controversies. Moral issues should be reported in a special book under certain titles, arranged without regard for order. An alphabetical index can be assigned to these later.

PART 4.

Special rules to be observed in the reading of the Fathers. Finally, in order that a person may be able to progress in reading the true and genuine writings of the Fathers with greater benefit and with dexterity of judgment, he should observe the following canons:

(1) In paraenetic and demegoric (that is, homiletical) matters, when the Fathers engaged more freely in rhetoric, none of their assertions should be pressed too literally.* Jerome (*adversus Helvid.*), excusing certain unhelpful things which he had said, writes: "We engaged in rhetoric and gave up something to our speeches." Theodoret (Dial. 3.): "I myself do not consider those things which are said panegyrically and rhetorically in the Church to be a rule of dogmas and decrees." Sixtus Senensis (lib. 6. *Biblioth. annos 152.*) advises: "The words of preachers are not always to be received with the same rigidity with which they first arrive at the ears, for they often express many things with hyperbole and are influenced either by the occasion of places, persons, or times, or they are caught up in a surge of emotions or by the course of their oration." Indeed, he concludes that this happened to Chrysostom on occasion.

Bellarmine (lib. 2. *de Missa* cap. 10.): "I say that Chrysostom said this by way of digression" (namely, that it is better not to take part in a sacrifice than to be present and not to sacrifice).

(2) In agonistics, polemics, and elenctics, when the Fathers were carried away by the intensity of the dispute and incited by zeal for defeating an adversary, they sometimes took hold of something for the defense of their case and bent it too far in the opposite direction. Tertullian, in order to uphold his case against Praxeas, seizes the opportunity whenever possible to prove that the Person of the Father differs from the Person of the Son, and at length he distinguishes them also by this mark, that "the Father is invisible, the Son visible," although it is obvious that Christ, in that He is God, is not distinguished from the Father by this mark.

---

*   *omnia illorum pronunciata non sint ad vivum resecanda*

Basil (*Epist. 64 de Gregorio Neocaesariensi*) writes this: "This saying of his that the Son and the Father are one 'in Person' was not said by way of decree, but because of contention." There is also this from Nicephorus (lib. 6. cap. 25. of the same epistle of Basil), where he writes: "Dionysius of Alexandria provided the first seed-bed for this wickedness which states the inequality of the Father and the Son, not by any sort of deviousness of mind and judgment, but because he wanted to attack Sabellius too vehemently and too sharply. Therefore, with too much zeal for contention, he fell into the opposite error. And although it would have been sufficient to point out that the person of the Father and the Son is not the same, Dionysius, in order to convict his adversary openly and thoroughly, alleged not only a distinction of Persons, but also a difference of substance and a change of glory, as if a remission of power."

Basil makes this point using an example of gardeners "who, in trying to straighten a crooked branch of a tender tree, often bend it too far in the opposite direction." Gennadius writes about the Roman bishop Julius' *Epistola de incarnatione Christi*: "Just as at first it seemed highly appropriate for refuting the Nestorians, who were trying to establish two persons in Christ, so a little later it was judged to be very unhelpful, and indeed harmful, because it seemed possible to defend the Eutychian madness."

Jerome thinks very highly of Tertullian in many areas, but when he was pressed with Tertullian's authority in the Helvidian controversy, he cried out with these words, "Tertullian is not a son of the Church!"

Erasmus judges thus concerning Jerome's disputations against Vigilantius, Jovinian and Helvidius: "He sometimes exceeds the limits of restraint and truth and praises with in-dignity the virginity of a spouse." Jerome (he says in *lib. adv. Piggium*) "was sometimes so carried away by fervent emotion in the admiration of virginity that marriage seemed injuri-ous even to godly men. This may be useless, except that those things are found in Jerome's writings which were condemned by that name in Tertullian."

Cornelius Mussus, bishop of Bitonto (in *Epist. Rom.* c. 5. p. 270.): "It is peculiar to Augustine that, when he fights against a certain error, he exaggerates it with so much inten-sity that he seems to provide an opening for the opposite er-ror. So when he rails against Arius, he seems to support Sabel-lius; when against Sabellius, he seems to support Arius; when against Pelagius, he seems to support the Manichaeans; when against the Manichaeans, he seems to support Pelagius." The same things are repeated by Harding. (art. 12. sect. 10.) and by Acosta (lib. 2. *de Christo revelato* cap. 29.) concerning Jerome. Thus, in the disputations against the Manichaeans, they speak rather unhelpfully of the powers of free will.

(3) In their exegetical writings, they certainly employ a calmer demeanor. But due to their ignorance of Hebrew, which is common to practically all of them except for Jerome, and because of an unhelpful translation of the Bible, they wander rather often and stray from the genuine sense of Scripture. Read the expositions of Augustine, Basil, and Cassiodorus on the Psalter, and it will be apparent how far they depart from the truth of the Hebrew text. Thus, when they render the rea-son why something was said or done in their exposition of a text, they rather often rely too freely on their own ingenuity. Chrysostom (in cap. 1. *Matth.*) asks: "Why did the angel not re-veal the conception of Christ to the Virgin after it had already

taken place, as he did to Joseph?" He then answers: "So that sadness might not consume the soul of this woman who was amazed and feeling ashamed. For it surely could happen that, unaware of such a great secret, she might discern something cruel about herself, and despising shameful fame as much as she cherished honesty, she might suddenly fly, either into joy or into a snare, etc." Euthymius follows Chrysostom, but it cannot be denied that Chrysostom here went too far, which Barradius himself acknowledges (tom. 1. *comm. in conc. Evang.* lib. 8. cap. 6.).

(4) In homiletical, exegetical, and didactic matters, they sometimes either pass by the literal, Scriptural sense or touch on it only briefly, descending immediately into allegories which are often harsh, forced, and untimely. Basil concludes more correctly (homil. 2. *hexaem.*, near the middle): "Let us postpone any further tropical and allegorical interpretation and understand the sense of darkness (of Genesis 1:2) simply, not inquisitively."

(5) In poetic writings, they indulge their ingenuity too freely and pursue the elegance of the verses rather than the accurate understanding of the Scripture. Responding to that which is presented from Prudentius, that "it is a festival for the criminal spirits under the Styx," Bellarmine says (libr. 2. *de purgatory.* cap. 18.): "I have no other response but that Prudentius was toying with a poetical custom."

The poetical figures which they sometimes employed in prose also pertain to this. Chemnitz (in *Theolog. Jesuit.* cap. 11. p. 102.): "Nazianzen, with his apostrophes that were more flowery and rhetorical than they were solid and theological, gave occasion for many superstitions." He says the same thing in *Orat. de lect. Patrum:* "Apostrophes were customarily used by

Nazianzen, so that he says: 'O great and sacred Pascha, for I speak with you!' But these figures of speech used in rhetorical discourses do not prove the invocation of the saints."

(6) They speak more securely before controversies have been instigated. Augustine responds to Julian the Pelagian, who was using certain sayings of the ancients (lib. 1. *contra Julian*. cap. 2.): "They spoke quite freely when that contest had not yet been instigated. When he was debating in the Catholic Church, he thought that he was understood in no other way; no one was disturbed by such a question, etc." Toletus (in *cap. 6. John*. annot. 20.): "Not only Chrysostom and Cyril, but also other teachers, especially the Greeks, grant too much to human free will, because the Pelagian heresy was not yet prowling around at that time, especially at the time of Chrysostom."

(7) They sometimes yield to the received custom of their times, no differently than a ship's captain yields and veers into the whirlpools in front of him, if he cannot hold a straight course without serious disturbance. Augustine (*Epist. 119. ad Januar.*): "I do not dare to condemn too freely many things of this kind which were done to avoid offending many individuals, either holy or unruly." He says the same (*lib. 20. contra Faustum* cap. 21.): "What we teach is one thing; what we put up with is another. And as long as we are in the process of correcting it, we are compelled to tolerate it."

(8) At times they attribute too much to uncertain rumors, and they seek forms of speaking from the common crowd. Melchior Canus (lib. 11. *Locor. commun.* cap. 6.): "We cannot deny that men who are otherwise very serious have both followed and reported in their writings to posterity certain rumors that had been spread, especially in describing the

wonders of the saints. In this matter, as it seems to me, they indulged either themselves or certainly the common crowd of the faithful too much. They sensed that this crowd not only readily believed those miracles, but also demanded them exceedingly, and that it pleased the noblest of authors that the true law of history was to write those things which were held to be true by the crowd, etc. I can perhaps justly and truly say the same things about Bede and Gregory."

Baronius (in *annal.* ann. 109. par. 49.) brings in from Hilduinus this excuse for Gregory of Tours: "Consideration should be shown to the simplicity of a religious man, Bishop Gregory of Tours, who, thinking differently than the truth suggests, commended many things in his writings, not from the cunning of deceit, but from a desire for kindness and simplicity." He says the same (ann. 44. par. 42.): "As for the deeds of the Apostles, after they have been separated one from another, the matter is equally obscure. For when either the deeds or the writings in the name of the Apostles are found to be counterfeits, or if some story that has been told about them by true and sincere writers does not remain whole and entirely uncorrupted, they simply throw the mind into a certain despair of ever being able to know what is true and certain."

To this pertains the fact that, in the histories, they follow the assertion and authority of their ancestors without any examination or discretion. This is where the story came from about Peter's episcopate in the city of Rome lasting 25 years.

(9) It must be carefully noted whether they are proposing and confirming some dogma by a formal profession and in the proper seat, or whether they are only touching on some-

thing along the way in passing. Likewise, whether they are debating from their own opinion or from the opinion of others; whether they declare something to be certain or only as probable. Jerome (in *apol. pro libr. contra Jovin.*): "It is one thing to write something gymnastically, another to assert something dogmatically." Joach. Abbas (in *revelat.*): "From conjectures, this can be said as a matter of opinion, not as a matter of understanding." The same goes for the testimonies of the Fathers in which they say that those two witnesses are Enoch and Elijah. He calls these, "not knowledge nor understanding, but opinions which can be mistaken." Otto Frisingensis (lib. 4. cap. 18.): "It must be considered according to what the authors are sayings, what is said by way of opinion, what is said by way of assertion." Casaubonus (in *notis ad Epist. Gregorii Nysseni ad Ambrosium et Basilissam* p. 89.): "Those who wish to read the Fathers beneficially should always remember that sometimes the Fathers speak in one way when they treat something didactically and seriously, and in another way when they treat something in passing and, as they themselves are wont to say, when they are serving their own purpose *economically.*" Thus Gregory of Nyssa and Jerome, when they deal with the undertaking of a pilgrimage to Jerusalem didactically and simply, refute the opinion of those who thought that there was more grace and virtue in those places than in other places where the divine Word is preached. But in other instances, and considering the circumstances, they seem to attribute something to those pilgrimages.

These things have been said concerning the reading of the Fathers, and they can easily be accommodated to reading the decrees of the Councils, where we commend the *Tomos Conciliorum a Severino Binio in quinque voluminibus Coloniae editos*, in which, nevertheless, the notes should be read with discretion.

CHAPTER 4.

THE READING OF THE SCHOLASTICS.

With grave and salutary deliberation, Blessed Luther eliminated Scholastic Theology from our schools and called us back only to the crystal-clear fountains of the Scriptures*. Therefore, it should the furthest thing from our minds that we would wish to bring it back into our theological department, as if it had a right to dwell among us, and to feed again on the acorns discovered among the crops,** especially since the experience of the previous centuries has taught sufficiently (and then some) how much darkness and what horrible corruptions of the heavenly doctrine were brought into the Church through Scholastic Theology. In order that greater discretion may be employed in this matter, we will divide the sins and errors of the Scholastics into certain classes, by which they seduced both themselves and others.

---

*   He writes (*lib. advers. Latomum*): "Scholastic Theology is nothing else but inane falsehood and ignorance of the truth."

**   Rupertus Gallus wrote 300 years ago, in a certain book of Lutetia which was published a hundred years ago, that it had been revealed to him in a vision that "the doctrine in the Church is as if a man who carried the purest and healthiest loaves of bread on his back, while meanwhile a starving man took up a stone in his hands and nibbled on it."

(1) *Concerning the principle of disputation.* They mixed philosophy with theology into a single chaos. Johannes Duns* (in libr. 3. sent. dist. 24. q. i.) asserts with eloquent words:"The theological doctors eventually mixed philosophy with theology, and with tremendous benefit." We admit that such a mixture, or rather, confusion, was made by them, but that it was done "with tremendous benefit" is shown to be false by the outcome itself, for they mixed them together in such a way that out of two things which are, in themselves, good, they made one very bad thing, like a bad cook who mixes many soups together. For this reason, Erasmus says (in *Moria*):"Scholastic Theology, from Sorbonne of the Parisians, was composed by means of a certain mixture of divine utterances and philosophical reasoning. It is a bi-form discipline, as if from the race of centaurs." The Sorbonnites, in a catalogue of the errors of the Master of Sentences, added as a footnote, rejected that confusion in the eloquent words of Thomas Aquinas, although they themselves commit that confusion elsewhere:"They say that he erred in many areas of his doctrine in that he applied too much the principles of philosophy, or rather certain words of the philosophers, to the conclusions of theology. For theologians should not speak in the same way as the philosophers speak, as Augustine teaches (10. *de. civ. Dei* cap. 23.), saying:'The philosophers speak with unrestrained words, nor are they afraid of offending religious ears in matters that are very hard to understand. But we must speak according to a certain standard. A lack of restraint in our words gives birth to a wicked opinion, even concerning the things which are meant by these words.'" They are absolutely right about that.

---

* Otherwise known as Scotus, whom they call 'the Doctor of Subtlety,' but is better called 'the Doctor of Darkness.' (σκότινος, scotinos, *a play on Scotus*)

Others, too, prior to the work of Reformation begun by Luther, rejected this mixture of philosophy with theology* among the Scholastics. Abbas Trithemicus says: "From that time when Scholastic Theology acquired strength in the Church, secular philosophy began to pollute sacred theology." The same complaint occurs in a book entitled *Onus Ecclesiae:* "The pagans seek to destroy the evangelical standard. Therefore, the devil encourages that the doctrine of Christians be supported with pagan authorities and that the dogmas of the pagans be mingled with the principles of the faith, so that at length the evangelical truth might be inflated from the inside with the deceit of the Sophists."

After the work of reformation was begun, Albert, Archbishop of Mainz**, Melchior Canus***, Longolius (in *oratione ad Lutheranos*) and others rejected the same things. Ambrosius Catharinus (Archbishop of Conza and assessor of the Council of Trent) contributes this eloquent statement in his writings against Domingo de Soto: "The Scholastics have placed Sacred Scripture behind their reason and philosophy, and therefore they have gone astray from the right path. The Fathers leaned more heavily on the Scriptures and relied on them. But the Scholastics rely more heavily on philosophy, so that, unsurprisingly, the Fathers did not go astray from the truth in this matter, but struck out against the Scholastics."

---

* μιξοφιλοσοφοθεολογίαν

** In a letter prefaced by the book of Erasmus entitled *De ratione perveniendi ad veram Theologiam.*

*** lib. 8. *locor. comm.* cap. 1 and lib. 9. cap. 1. He says: "It turns out that I see myself saying, with great agreement on the part of everyone, that the doctrine of the Schola is wretched. It philosophizes concerning divine matters, having removed the authority from Holy Scripture with its twisted syllogisms."

Ludov. Vives has much to say (lib. 21. *de civ. Dei* cap. 7.) in assessing this confusion of the distinct sciences: "Since this whole topic of resurrection, judgment, the punishments of the wicked, and the blessedness of the godly exceeds the limits and grasp of Nature, the remarkable Scholastic Theologians Thomas, Scotus, Occam, Henrico Gandavens, Durandus and Paludanus discuss and define all those things from Aristotelian dogmas and tenaciously fight among themselves, armed only with the arguments of Nature, such as when they ask if bodies will be resurrected, if it will take place at the end of the world, if the material that at one time adorned the human form always longs for that same form, if the souls of the blessed are able to suffer, if the movement of the heavens will be stilled and in what position of the heavens it will be stilled, etc., and six hundred other things which they dispute philosophically, so that you would think they were pagan Athenians, not Parisian Christians."

To this pertains the fact that they draw their conclusions in the lofty mysteries of the faith from the principles of logic, physics, metaphysics, etc., having either passed by or lightly touched on the words of Scripture, so that you hear Aristotle more often than the Apostle in those disputations, although the saner form of philosophy rejects this *change to another genre*[*] and instead requires a homogeneity of points. If, for the sake of form, they introduce the Scripture, they follow a very corrupt Latin translation, leaving out the fountains, since they were ignorant of both the Hebrew and the Greek alphabets. The most famous is that sentence for the commendation of order in Rom. 13:1, "Whatever things exist have been ordained by God," although in Greek it should be read far dif-

---

[*]   lib. 1. *poster.* c. 7.

ferently, "The authorities that exist have been established by God."

They also violently and plainly twist the Scriptures outside their aim, embellishing them with foreign meanings. Erasmus (in *com. Theolog.* p. 191.): "Some recklessly drag the divine Scripture to an utterly foreign sense, like the man who has taken what is said in Habakkuk about the tents of the enemy, that 'the skins of the land of Midian will tremble,' and distorted it to refer to the flaying of Bartholomew, about which there is a story, although it lacks credibility. Or there is the man who took that statement from the book of Judith, 'going around the valley, they came to the gate,' and foolishly bent it around to the arguments of the four books of Peter Lombard, who wrote the theological sentences, and he wants that which is even more subtle in this passage to be, in the same words, an allusion to his own name and nickname." Thomas of Argentina (in *prolog. super 2. sentient.*) transfers the saying from Judges 1:15, "he gave her the upper and lower springs," to the article of creation. Therefore, we justly say the same thing about the back-rests of the Papal See, namely, the Scholastics, that Aventinus says (lib. 7. *Annal. Bojorum de Gregorio VII.*), "he forced a false interpretation on the divine writings, so that they might serve his own fancy."

They dispute from the sayings of the Fathers as if from the proper principle of theology, and they regard their authority to be equal with the authority of Scripture, although the Fathers themselves, in their own eloquent and clear words, refused to be dragged away to that sublime height of authority. Thomas, indeed, says (p. 1. q. 1. art. 8.): "The sacred doctrine uses the authorities of other doctors of the Church, not as if arguing from proper sources, but from probable sources." But in practice, this is not observed among the Scholastics. For they sometimes cite the sayings of the ancients in truncated and corrupt form, from books that have been adulterated and forged. Thus Gratianus, a contemporary and brother of Lombard, cites (c. *In canonicis* dist. 10.) this sentence from Augustine, "The decretal epistles of the popes should be numbered among the canonical Scriptures," which never entered the mind of Augustine. Bellarmine, in attempting to excuse the disgraceful behavior of Gratianus, responds (libr. 2. *de council.* cap. 12.): "Gratianus was deceived by a distorted manuscript of Augustine, since the true and corrected manuscripts of Augustine read much differently."

(2) *Concerning the object of disputation.* As they err in discussing principles theologically, so they also err in the very object of disputation. For they propose *idle, curious, thorny, useless, absurd, superstitious,* and sometimes even *wicked* questions, wherefore Nicol. de Clemangis justly writes: "The doctrine of the Scholastics has the same nature as the fruits that grew around the tar pits of Sodom; even though they externally provide a certain delightful splendor to the eyes, nevertheless, they are inwardly only dust and ashes." The Apostle defines theology in Titus 1:1 as "the knowledge of the truth which is according to godliness," and therefore anything that is neither necessary for knowing the truth nor pertaining to godliness should not be considered a theological axiom or problem. On the contrary, he gravely commands in 2 Tim. 2:16: "Shun profane and idle babblings, for they will increase unto more ungodliness." And in verse 23: "But avoid foolish and unlearned questions, knowing that they generate strife." With these words from Romans 12:3, he also restrains the curiosity of human ingenuity in searching out the things that have not been revealed: "Not to

think beyond what it is proper to think, but to think toward thinking soberly." But the Scholastic doctors forgot these apostolic admonitions, for they promote the kinds of questions that do nothing either for knowing the truth or for instilling a zeal for piety.

Ludov. Vives complains about this (in *comment. libr. 20. August. de civ. Dei* cap. 16.), for when Augustine humbly said, "I think that no one knows what hellfire is like or where in the world it is," Vives adds, "No one? You did not take part in the battles with the Scholastics, where there is no one, either Batalarius or Magistellus, who does not know that hellfire is that elemental fire whose home lies between the air and the globe of the moon, namely, that it will come down and purge the remaining three elements with its flame! If you do not approve of this, there will be no lack of those who religiously swear that the fire will come from the flames of the sun's rays, kindled in mid-air as the dense and burning-hot rays come together, as onto a sunken mirror made of steel. But it is no wonder, for fire was not in use in your time as much as it is now, since the Philosophers—that I may set aside the Theologians—whether in mid-December or in mid-July, pull and twist nothing but fire from their mouth, hands, and feet. Theologians are made from philosophers, and the holier ones even transfer this method of philosophizing into the schools, because it is far easier for them to define hellfire than it is for you and your equals, etc."

Erasmus (in *annotate. 1 Timoth. 1.* p. 463.) likewise has woven together a lengthy complaint concerning those questions of the Scholastics: "Things that have no end include practically all the things that now belong to the vulgar theologians. For the more of these little questions there are, the more also spring forth from never-ending opportunities, of which, if you

produce a billion of them, there would still be more leftover."
And afterwards: "How many examinations of questions shall
we take up concerning Baptism, concerning the Synaxis, concerning the sacrament of penance, several of which are of such
a kind that it is of no great importance to know, and even as
they can be asserted emphatically, so they also cannot be refuted or proven, etc.?* What should I now say about questions
which are not only highly unnecessary, but almost, I might say,
wicked, which we promote about the power of God, about the
power of the Roman popes, etc.? We could adduce six hundred
questions of this kind from the Scholastics. This is how idle
the questions are: In the state of innocence, would there have
been an equal number of men and women? Would all people
have been born in the masculine gender? Would children in
the state of innocence have been born with perfect use of reason? Would reproduction have taken place through sexual re-
lations? Would there have been integrity with birth, etc.?" They
are *curious* questions: "What will the fire be like by which the
world will be destroyed? How big, wide, and deep is the fiery
heaven? Is there dancing there? Is it bright enough? What was
God doing before the world was formed?" They are *thorny* questions: "Could God understand certain things distinctly, if He
had no distinct relationship of reason toward them? Could He
produce a consideration without foundation and boundary?
Could He cause an angel to shape matter? Could He produce a
universal Nature without individuals, etc.?" They are *useless*: "Is
the nature of the universe more capable of being united than
human nature? Should Adam have been an incarnate man?
Was the formation of the flesh of Christ of a man and a woman fitting? Would it have been more fitting of a man?" They are

---

*   In *Meth. Theol.* p. 34. he calls them "curious and thorny trickery
and abstinent anxieties of questions."

absurd: "Could the Son of God or should the Son of God have assumed the nature of an ass, a serpent, a dove? Could God have substituted a woman in the place of Christ? Does an ass drink Baptism, if he drinks consecrated water? Would it have been a valid formula if Christ had instituted it in the name of Buff Baff?" They are *superstitious:* "If a mouse nibbles on the consecrated host, does it nibble on the body of Christ? Is the body of the Lord in the body of a mouse caught in a mouse-trap to be worshiped? What should be done with that mouse? Should it be disemboweled and the consecrated host that is found in it offered to a believer to eat?" (See Holderus' *Murem exenteratum et petitorium exhortatorium,* etc.) They are *ungodly:* "Is the proposition, 'God the Father hates the Son,' possible? Could God have substituted the devil in the place of Christ? If God had substituted a gourd, how would it have preached? How would it do miracles? How could it be crucified? Would a Baptism be effective if it were consecrated in the name of the devil? Could the pope repeal something that was decreed by the Apostles? Is he a simple man, or is he like God, or does he participate in both natures with Christ, etc.?"

(3) *Concerning the manner of disputation.* Finally, as they sin greatly in the principle and object, so also in the manner of disputation. For first, there is an immense and obvious desire among all of them to contradict one another, so that a consensus can hardly be found among two or three of them in any question. The Parisian theologian Wesselus lamented this long ago, as Flacius reports (in *libr. de sectis, dissidiis et dissens. Pontif.* p. 78.). Roffensis acknowledges, in a book against Luther, that the Scholastics fight with one another over that question, "Is man capable of willing anything good without special help from God?" Ludovic. Vives (in *18. August. de civ. Dei* cap. 18.):

"The Scholastics dispute whether the power to create can be communicated to a creature, about which Thomas says many things, whose arguments Scotus strives to weaken in order to confirm his own, which Occamus tries to undermine in order to strengthen his own. But Petrus Aliacensis also diminishes these arguments, to the point that they are either playing around in a serious matter, or they force a heavenly matter to become subservient to their feelings and factions. Which morals can be corrected? Which tiny passions can be restrained and removed? Who can be made divine from a doctrine that, for the sake of pleasing human passions, has been stirred up with strife, and dragged, and turned up and down, and beaten with the devices of those who quarrel so stubbornly?"

Erasmus (*contra Latomum*): "The Scholastics do not all think the same, nor are they all free from error. For those who follow Thomas dissent from those who follow Scotus; they practically regard them as heretics." He says the same (in *Enchirid. milit. Christ.*): "But what do we think will happen if we set forth Occamus, or Durandus, or Scotus, or Gabrieles, or Alvaro to the Turks as they embrace Christ? What will they think? Or what will they feel (for they, too, are certainly men, if nothing else) when they hear those thorny and inextricable word tricks, etc., especially when they see that there is no agreement, even among those great professors of religion, so that they frequently contend with one another to the point of pallor, to the point of insults, to the point of spitting, and sometimes even to the point of blows, where the preachers practice hand-to-hand and also long-range combat for the sake of their Thomas, where the Minorites guard against the subtle and Seraphic doctors, joined at the elbow, where some speak as Nominalists, others as Realists?"

Lombard, the father of the Scholastics, is condemned in many areas by more recent writers with this formula added: "Here the Master is not supported."

The Parisians likewise condemn many things in Thomas Aquinas and add: "It seems presumptuous so to extol his doctrine above all other doctors, that one is not allowed to believe or to claim that he erred in the faith, or to oppose his canonization, as some pretend with great outward show." In *Chronico Henrici de Erphordia* there is a Bull of Bishop Stephan of Paris in which this bishop testifies: "Many bishops have condemned Thomas' doctrine." When he could not otherwise protect him, Aegidius of Rome writes, "His books have been corrupted by know-nothings and spiteful men," and for this reason he changes, corrects, or mitigates more than a few things in Thomas' books; this work is called *Correctorium Thomae*. See Flacius (*de sectis* p. 124. et seqq.).

Secondly, they dispute topically and skeptically the things that have been defined in the Holy Scriptures, and, in this way, they introduce academic *epoché* into a passage of certain reliability and full assurance. Tossed about by various arguments, as by waves, now in this direction, now in that, they do not know, finally, where to retreat, and so they conclude by leaving the matter in doubt. "If you wish to pass over to this opinion, respond in this way to the opposing arguments. If you prefer to pass over to another, then respond in this way." When many objections have been proposed, they sometimes add: "If you are looking for a way out, let him reply who is able, 'Here it is limited, etc.'" They ask about grace, about the effect of Baptism, about Justification, etc., introducing probable arguments on both sides. When Gratianus (at the end of dist. 1. *de poenit.*) has introduced diverse authorities for confession and satisfaction, he adds: "To which of these one should rather adhere is left to the judgment of the reader, for both sides have supporters, wise and religious men."

Thirdly, however, when it comes to reserved questions which are not defined in the Scriptures and are often placed beyond the grasp of reason, they boldly go on to define them. Ludov. Vives (in *lib. 13. de civ. Dei* cap. 1.): "Here they ask many things about what would have happened if man had not fallen. The more recent of them, the ones who wrote commentaries on the Sentences, confidently define whatever comes into their mind, sometimes by means of arbitrary conjectures, sometimes by reasoning sought from the nature of things. I hear their reasons, but I see plainly that they are walking about in darkness, nor do they wish to proceed slowly or feeling their way about, but they rush forth in whichever way they are leaning, with no fear of the cliffs. Concerning the ranks of angels, concerning the fiery heaven, etc."

They dispute so boldly that someone may justly ask how recently they fell down from heaven! They discuss the nature of hellfire and the chambers of hell, etc., so artfully that they might seem to have gone forth from the pit of the abyss with the locusts of Revelation (Rev. 9:34).

They use obscure terms, foreign words, and they always act in such a way that the things which are difficult, they render more difficult with their thorny questions, while the things that are clear they envelope in obscure wrappings of questions and in horrible-sounding riddles of words. From here are heard the conflicts over *thisness, homineity, femineity**, etc. Nothing is heard more often than *subjectibility, passionability, po-*

---

*   *haecceitas, homineitas, foemineitas*

tentiality, susceptibility, componibility, aptitudinability. They stir up cries of *singularizations, effectuations, meliorizations, specifications, infinitations.* They pierce the ears with *dabilible, proferibilible, fixibilible, meliorabilible, verificabilible, specificabilible, exemplificabilible* corollaries.

This alone should be pondered, with what labyrinths of questions they have enveloped the article of the Trinity, with what monstrosities of words they have polluted that lofty mystery of faith. This is how they have expressed 'Person': "He does not call it a relationship of origin, not a common relationship, but a double negation of communicability in genus, not meaning something positive and a prime intention outside the genus, not implying a second circumincession which is a mutual distinction of the one subsisting in a real sense in the one subsisting by an assistance of presentiality in the same essence."

More examples of the manner of disputation used by the Scholastics can be seen in Binderus (in *Theolog. Scholastica*) and in Dr. Meisner (in *dissertate. Tubingae habita*), etc.

Even so, we do not strenuously object if someone thinks he can obtain some benefit from the reading of the Scholastics, as long as the following canons are observed:

(1) No one should approach the reading of the Scholastics before he has first acquired for himself a solid and accurate knowledge of genuine theology from the Holy Scriptures. Otherwise, he will float about, wandering from here to there, washed away by the whirlpools of various opinions.

(2) It is also required that he be well-versed in the reading of the Greek and Latin Fathers. For since the Scholastics frequently cite the sayings of the Fathers, which they mostly

bring in from the collections of others or from corrupt versions, one must diligently pay attention where and in what ways they depart from the mind of the Fathers.

(3) Certain classes of Scholastics should be established, since they are not all of the same *age, authority,* or *authenticity.* The *first age* of Scholastics began around the year 1000 and lasted until the year 1220. They often rely on badly distorted sentences of the Fathers to prove theological questions. The most prominent of them is Lombard, called the Master of Sentences.[*] The *second age* began around the year 1220 and lasted until the year 1330. They disputed concerning the articles of faith from philosophical principles. Thomas is the most outstanding among them. The *last age* began in 1330 and lasted until the year 1517, at which time Blessed Luther began the work of Reformation. They enlarged the errors and proved their conclusions from the pontifical decrees. Thus, although Gabriel Biel (in *lectionibus super canonem Missae* lect. 57.) confirmed with many arguments that "the indulgences of the Pope do not benefit the souls in purgatory," nevertheless, after his book went out, he saw the Bulls of Sixtus IV and Innocent VIII, who gave indulgences directly to the dead, and he retracted the things that he had taught at first, as Carolus Molinoeus reports (in *orat. Tübing. habita*).

They can also be distinguished into the groups of *Sententionaries, Summists,* and *Quodlibetarians.*

---

[*] Aventinus (lib. 6. *annal.*): "Lombard published four books of theologoumena, but the truth and the purest fount of most holy philosophy, as I have received a thousand times more from Jac. Fabrus and Jodocus Clichtovaeus, he has confounded with the mud of his questions and with the rivulets of his opinions."

(4) No one should journey into that whole, vast, winding, convoluted sea; he should only sample some things from it around the foremost edges, firmly convinced that the Sacred Scriptures alone are the immovable, perfect, and certain rule of our faith, from which he is convinced that, if he wishes to make a digression to the others, even so he cannot hope to gain as much fruit from the reading of the Scholastics as he can by the reading of the ancient Fathers.

Erasmus (in *com. Theol.* p. 34.): "If a person puts together those ancient theologians—Origen, Basil, Chrysostom, Jerome—side by side with these more recent Scholastics and compares them, he will see that there, among the Fathers, flows a golden river, while here, among the Scholastics, flow certain little brooks which are neither very pure nor do they correspond to their fountain. There the oracles of divine truth thunder; here the bare little tricks of men; the more closely you inspect them, the more similar they appear to dreams. There the building, resting on the solid foundations of the Scriptures, rises up to the heights; here the machine, no less vain than it is monstrous, built up with the futile devices or even adulations of men, is carried away into the immense. There you will be both delighted and amply filled as in the most fruitful gardens; while here you will be tortured and torn to pieces among the sterile thorns. There all things are full of majesty; here there is nothing splendid, but much that is sordid, and little that is worthy of the dignity of theology."

(5) It is sufficient, therefore, to run through Lombard's *Libri Sententiarum*, Thomas' *Summa*, the *Commentarii* of Bonaventure and Biel (who compiled the rest).

(6) If any useful distinctions come to mind, clear arguments, etc., they should be reported in their proper place in the books, namely, in the collections mentioned above. The idle, curious and superstitious questions should be left out.

(7) Lombard, Thomas, and others judge more correctly in some things than the modern Papists do. Therefore, those things should be diligently noted, that they may be used against the Papists.

(8) The arguments which occur in the controversial questions between us and the Papists should be accurately observed, for the Papists borrow those things from themselves, but almost nothing will come up, to which another of the Scholastics, on account of their perpetual, malignant need to contradict, has not already responded.

CORONIS ON TEMPTATION.

Three things are meant with the term *temptation*, which, when added to *prayer* and *meditation*, adds a sort of complement and perfection to theological study.

(1) *A spiritual sense and experience.* Luther says: "Temptation teaches one not only to know, but also to sense and to experience the certainty, truth, sweetness, power, and comfort of the Word." Epiphanius, in restraining the untimely allegories of Origen, says: "Not all the divine words demand an allegory, but should be understood as they are. They do demand insight and experience* to know the power of each hypothesis." Dr. Chemnitz (in praef. *locor.*) understands this "insight" to be a consideration of order and the distinction of the parts in the whole corpus of doctrine, and he take the "experience" to be the sense and experience of the godly in the use of doctrine, in penitence, fear, faith, invocation, proper comforts. This is understood in the exercises of piety. Therefore, David's admonition applies here from Psalm 34:9: "Taste and see how sweet the Lord is! Blessed is the man who hopes in Him."

It is not enough, then, to know *theoretically* that God is just, and that, in the Law, He accuses and condemns sins, but one must also experience *practically*, in the exercise of true penitence, that God is seriously angry over sins. It is not enough to know *theoretically* that God is merciful and that, in the Gospel,

---

*   θεορία καὶ αἴσθησις

He forgives the sins of the penitent for the sake of Christ the Mediator, but one must also experience *practically*, in the exercises of faith and invocation, the goodness and mercy of God. The Psalm calls this "tasting how sweet the Lord is." Taste consists in sense and experience; so, too, the spiritual taste of the soul embraces spiritual sense and experience. It is not enough to know *theoretically* that eternal life is prepared for the godly and believing, but one must also know *practically* some foretaste of that life through the Holy Spirit, which the Epistle to the Hebrews, in 6:4, calls "to taste the heavenly gift and to be made a partaker of the Holy Spirit;" v. 5, "to taste the good Word of God and the powers of the coming age."

This *experience* of the Word is obtained through serious meditation and prayer, wherefore Bernard piously says about the manner of prayer (col. 1252.): "Reading occurs first, like a foundation, and after the material has been given, it sends you on to mediation. But meditation seeks more carefully what is to be desired, and, as if digging for a treasure, it finds it and points to it. But since it is not strong enough to obtain it by itself, it sends us to prayer. Prayer, as it raises itself with all its strength to the Lord, obtains the desirable treasure, the sweetness of contemplation. And when this comes, it repays the work of three preachers as it drenches the thirsty soul with the sweetness of heavenly rain." (See the treatise, *On the Interpretation of Scripture*, par. 218.)

(2) *Patience under the cross.* While it is true that many adversities befall all the godly in this world, theologians especially and the faithful ministers of the Church are exposed to various weapons of calamity, since the devil is particularly hostile to them, as they bring no small defeat to his kingdom. Here, therefore, the admonition of Sirach 2:1 applies: "My son,

if you come near to serve the Lord, prepare your soul for temptation. Set your heart in order and endure." All those adversities are so diverse that they really cannot be listed one by one. For there are manifest persecutors, there are hidden detractors, there are false brothers, there are disobedient hearers, at times one must wrestle with the hatred of the world, at other times with a shortage of goods, etc. In 2 Cor. 4:8–10, Paul says about himself and the other authentic ministers of the Word: "In all things we suffer tribulation, but we are not in distress; we are cast into hardships, but we do not despair; we suffer persecution, but we are not forsaken; we are struck down, but we are not confounded, always carrying about in the body the death of Jesus." 1 Cor. 4:11–13: "To this hour we both hunger and thirst, and we are naked, and stricken with blows, and are vagabonds...We are cursed, we suffer persecution, we are blasphemed...We have been made as the filth of this world." (Add to this 2 Cor. 6:4, 11:23, etc.) Therefore, the mind must be fortified, and when adversities strike, we must not "think it strange concerning the fiery trial which comes upon us to try us, as though some strange thing were happening to us" (1 Pet. 4:12). But let us reflect on the fact that the cross and troubles are sent upon us for our good by the singular counsel of God (Psa. 119:71, Isa. 28:19). Let us weigh the divine promises of God's presence and help in troubles (Psa. 91:15, Isa. 43:2). Let us recall the lot which Christ, the Prophets, and the Apostles obtained in this world, nor let us expect for ourselves any peculiar fortune of our own (Mat. 5:12, 10:24; John 15:20). Let us ponder the fact that "our light and momentary tribulation is working a far more exceeding and eternal weight of glory in us who do not contemplate the things that are seen, but that are unseen" (2 Cor. 4:17, Acts 14:21, Rom. 8:18).

It would be most useful to write down quickly from the sayings of the Scripture the sources of the consolations that are to be contrasted with particular troubles and to place them under certain titles so that they are visible to us at first glance, if we are brought down into the school of the cross and are forced to experience this or that calamity. For it happens more often to those who are the most skilled that when those comforting passages are needed most, they do not come to mind. Psalm 119:22: "The rulers sat and spoke against me. But Your servant was trained in Your statues." V. 78: "A little way off, and they would have consumed me in the earth. But I will train in Your commandments." V. 92: "Unless Your Law had been my comfort, I would have perished in my affliction."

(3) *Perseverance in the zeal for piety.* The godly theologian is not only incited and tempted toward sins externally, through adversities, but also internally, through depraved suggestions, so that he is forced to experience the truth of that Apostolic pronouncement in 2 Cor. 7:5: "Fears within, fightings without." For the devil incites him to doubt the truth of the Word, the grace of God, providence, etc., to apostasy, to various sins, avarice, security, drunkenness, etc., especially to that most noxious and common disease, the chief source of all evils in the Church, namely, *ambition* and *pride.* One must resist these temptations with the strength of the Spirit, with meditation on the Word and with pious prayer, that we may be victorious in that perilous duel with Satan.

It would require too lengthy an effort to deal with each one of those temptations. We advise in general, therefore, that whenever the devil incites us to sin, one must reflect, on the one hand, (i) *on God's justice;* (ii) *on the shamefulness, the dreadfulness, and the damnable nature of sin;* (iii) *on the brief and momentary pleasure of sin; (iv) on the seriousness and eternal nature of the penalties of hell.* On the other hand, one must reflect (i) *on the fatherly goodness of God,* who has lavished on us so many benefits that it invites us to filial obedience; (ii) *on the beauty, dignity, and utility of furnishing obedience to God;* (iii) *on the brevity of enduring toils and labors in this battle;* (iv) *on the unspeakable sweetness of heavenly joy and on the eternity that never ends.*

The mind must be fortified against pride by means of meditation (i) *on the humility of Christ,* who humbled Himself for us up to the death of the cross. Augustine (serm. 39. *de verb. Dom.*): "Deign to be humble for God's sake, for God deigned to be humble for your sake." (ii) *On our neediness.* The maximum of the things that we know is the minimum of the things that we don't know. Whatever we have came down to us from the hand of God. Therefore, it is a foreign treasure. (iii) *On our fragility.* In temptation, we can easily succumb, unless divine grace preserves us. "God resists the proud, but gives grace to the humble" (1 Pet. 5:5). (v) *On foreign preeminence.* The gifts of God must be acknowledged in others, lest we do wrong to the Giver Himself. It does no harm if you submit to all men, but it does much harm if you place yourself ahead of even one. Confer the twelve rules of Giovanni Pico della Mirandola to be observed in spiritual battle (tom. 1. *operum* p. 210. edit. Bas.).

These things have now been said concerning the proper institution, the proper continuation, and the proper completion of theological study. May the most gracious God, the Author of all good, cause all things to yield to the glory of His name and to the benefit of our studies. Amen.

254

www.ingramcontent.com/pod-product-compliance
Lightning Source LLC
Chambersburg PA
CBHW060044100426

42742CB00014B/2697